Gran Canaria

Travel and tourism

Author
Sam Kennedy

Copyright Notice

Copyright © 2017 Global Print Digital
All Rights Reserved

Digital Management Copyright Notice. This Title is not in public domain, it is copyrighted to the original author, and being published by **Global Print Digital**. No other means of reproducing this title is accepted, and none of its content is editable, neither right to commercialize it is accepted, except with the consent of the author or authorized distributor. You must purchase this Title from a vendor who's right is given to sell it, other sources of purchase are not accepted, and accountable for an action against. We are happy that you understood, and being guided by these terms as you proceed. Thank you

First Printing: 2017.

ISBN: 978-1-912483-04-4

Publisher: Global Print Digital.
Arlington Row, Bibury, Cirencester GL7 5ND
Gloucester
United Kingdom.
Website: www.homeworkoffer.com

Table of Content

Introduction 1
Gran Canaria 4
   Geography of Gran Canaria 4
   History of Gran Canaria 5
   Government of Gran Canaria 7
   Economy & Industries 9
   The Environment in 11
      Plant Life in Gran Canaria 12
   Tourism 15
The People and Culture 18
Tour, Travel Tourism: Vacation, Holiday, Honeymoon 25
   Gran Canaria, the Children's Choice 31
   Tourism Information Offices 33
   What to See 36
      North Coastal and Inland 38
         City of Las Palmas 39
            Vegueta 41
            Triana 43
            Ciudad Jardín 46
            Santa Catalina 48
            Playa de las Canteras 50
            La Isleta 52
         Santa María de Guía 53
         Gáldar 54
         Agaete 57
         Puerto de las Nieves 58
         Arucas 59
         Firgas 61
         Moya 62
         Valleseco 63
         Teror 64
      South to West 65
         Meloneras 67
         Maspalomas 70
         Playa del Inglés 73
         Pasito Blanco 75

- Arguineguín 76
- Puerto de Mogán 77
- Puerto Rico 78
- Mogán 80
- San Nicolás de Tolentino 81
- Puerto de la Aldea 83
- East to South 84
  - Telde 85
  - Valsequillo 87
  - Ingenio 88
  - Agüimes 89
  - Barranco de Guayadeque 90
  - Santa Lucía de Tirajana 91
  - San Bartolomé de Tirajana 93
  - Fataga 95
- Central 96
  - Tafira 97
  - Jardín Botánico 98
  - Caldera de Bandama 100
  - Santa Brígida 101
  - Vega de San Mateo 102
  - Pico del Pozo de las Nieves 103
  - Cruz de Tejeda 105
  - Artenara 106
- *What to Do* *107*
  - Beaches 109
    - Las Canteras 111
    - Playa de las Alcaravaneras 112
    - Playa de San Agustín 113
    - Playa del Inglés 114
    - Maspalomas 116
    - Playa de Puerto Rico 117
    - Playa de Amadores 119
    - Playa de Mogán 120
    - Playa Taurito 122
    - Playa Meloneras 122
  - Leisure & Sports 124
    - Leisure 126
      - Walking & Hiking 128
      - Camel Safari 130

- Horse riding..130
- Rock Climbing 131
- Karting..133
- Fun & Theme Parks 134
- Sport 146
- Nightlife 158
- Culture 160
  - The Island Cultural Centre 161
  - Museums 163
    - Casa de Colón (Columbus House) 164
    - Centro Atlántico de Arte Moderno 165
    - Museo Canario...166
    - Casa Museo de Pérez Galdós 168
    - Pueblo Canario, Museo Néstor 169
- Eating Out 170
- Shopping 173
- Others Things to Do..175
  - Explore Vegueta, the old town of Las Palmas 175
  - Bandama Caldera...176
  - Hike to the impressive Roque Nublo 177
  - Paddle surfing in Gran Canaria 178
  - Spend the day at Palmitos Park 179
  - Spend the day exploring the Jardin Canario 180
  - Visit the historic Catedral de Santa Ana 181

What's On and Lively 182
- Around the Island 184
- Las Palmas 189

Where to Stay..194
- Gran Canaria Hotels...197

Travel Information 201
- When to get to Gran Canaria 202
- How to get to Gran Canaria 203
  - Airport (LPA) 204
- What to Bring along 209
- Getting Around 210
  - Airport Transfer 210
  - Gran Canaria Taxis 211
  - Car Hire 212

Driving in Gran Canaria	213
Necessary Info	*215*
Currency	216
Opening Hours in Gran Canaria	217
Electricity Information	218
Time & Water	219
Dangers and Nuisances	220
Health	222
Emergency Telephone Numbers	223
Communications	224
Speaking Spanish	225
The Gay & Lesbian	228
Disabled Facilities	229
Weather	*231*
Annual Average Temperatures for Gran Canaria	232

Introduction

Introduction to Canaria Tourism

Conquered by the Spanish and later invaded by masses of European vacationers, Gran Canaria is a mix of cultures and landscapes. Singing to the same seasonal rhythm as the Mediterranean, the third largest and most populated of the seven Canary Islands harbors lush, rolling meadows in the north and flat dusty plains and sandy beaches in the south, all in a fist-shaped island roughly the same size as the city of Houston. The capital, Las Palmas, is a popular port-of-call for large cruise liners, and provides two urban beaches for its dense population.

Things to do: Many visitors come for the incredibly healthy climate and invigorating mountain walks such as those found in the Roque Nublo Park. Others delve deep into the history in the historic old quarter of Las Palmas. But most seek little more than sun, sand and sea; bronzing on one of the island's 60 beaches. This is occasionally forsaken for strolls in pretty villages such as Tejeda, or a splash in one of the water parks of the south, where at night the revelry continues amidst scores of bars and clubs.

Restaurants and Dining: Pick your way past the dozens of British eateries in the main resorts and you'll find the local hangouts where goat's cheese, rabbit and veal are offered in various guises. Pork and chicken is also popular, served either grilled or roasted and almost always with papas arrugadas and mojo sauce--boiled potatoes in sea salt and a spicy pepper sauce. Unsurprisingly, the coastline is awash with good seafood restaurants. Parrot fish is a common catch and sea bream a local specialty.

Shopping: Shopping is a hugely popular sport in Gran Canaria, largely due to the reduced import taxes, making certain goods like alcohol, tobacco, electronics and perfumes cheaper than other places in Europe. For more poignant souvenirs grab a basket made out of banana leaves, local pottery and lace embroidery, or a miniature replica of the famous Canary Island wooden balconies. Las Palmas provides the most varied retail therapy with a smorgasbord of retailers lining streets such as Calle Mayor Triana and coloring the plentiful local markets.

Nightlife and Entertainment: Playa del Inglés is the winter party capital of Europe, especially popular with gay travelers. The Yumbo

Center is at the heart of the gay club land action offering a heady mixture of hardcore dance venues, drag shows and same sex bars. Check out the nearby Kasbah Center for family fun pubs. The capital, Las Palmas, also boasts a moonlight buzz.

Gran Canaria
Geography of Gran Canaria

Gran Canaria, along with Tenerife, is located in the centre of the Canarian archipelago. The round island so called because of its circular shape is 47 km (29 miles) across and covers an area of 1,560 sq km. Its highest peak, Pozo de Las Nieves (1,949m/6,431 ft above sea level), is situated right in the centre of the island.

Gran Canaria belongs to an area of the Atlantic Ocean, known as Macaronesia, which includes the Canary Islands as well as the archipelagos of Madeira, Azores and Cape Verde. The nearest point on the African coast is approximately 210 km (131 miles) away, while Cádiz, the closest port on the European continent, lies about 1250 km (781 miles) north of Gran Canaria.

Gran Canaria, which is the third largest island of the Canaries, boasts 236 km (approximately 147 miles) of coast with sandy beaches, predominantly concentrated in the southeast. This is where you'll find the famous beaches of Playa del Inglés and Maspalomas with its amazing sand dunes. Cliffs dominate the south western and western coasts, whereas the coastline of the north and northeast offers more diverse pleasures, including a wide variety of beaches and coves. The mountainous centre of the island features a few high peaks and many gorges radiating out towards the sea.

Coves and beaches, impressive cliffs, hidden corners, magnificent mountains, stunning craters and amazing ravines with their lush, sub-tropical vegetation and natural reserves represent some of the many natural delights, which mark Gran Canaria's personality ... a land of many faces.

History of Gran Canaria

There is a lot of myth and legend surrounding the early history of the Canary Islands, with many early inhabitants believing them to be the lost land of Atlantis. Others considered the islands to be the site of the magical, mystical Fortunate Islands, the blissful paradise of both Celtic and Greek mythology.

It is believed that Gran Canaria was already populated in around 500 B.C., although there are several theories regarding the origins of its early inhabitants. One widely accepted theory is that Gran Canaria's natives, widely known as Guanches although Canarios is actually the correct historical term, originally came from North Africa and that they were descendants of the Berber people. The Guanches lived very primitively as the unsophisticated tools and weapons found on the island bear witness to mostly in caves. Guanches are also believed to have used rocks and stones to build small structures for shelter. These make-shift dwellings would be covered with a roof of branches and leaves. Their most civilised achievement was earthenware, modelled without the use of a potter's wheel.

After the fall of the Roman Empire, Europe forgot about the Canary Islands for almost 1,000 years and until the rediscovery of the Canaries by Mediterranean sailors in the early 14th century, the 30,000 Guanches on the island of Gran Canaria lived a relatively peaceful life. This then changed drastically, in the 14th century, as the Italians, Portuguese and Catalans sent their ships to the islands to bring back slaves and furs. At the beginning of the 15th century, the rapid process of the conquest of the islands began.

In Gran Canaria, the Guanches fiercely resisted the Spanish invasion but, by 1483 Pedro de Vera, who led the Spanish forces, had completed the conquest, begun by Juan Rejón five years earlier. Many Guanches were killed or committed suicide rather than surrender to the Spanish. Those who survived were forced into slavery and to convert to Christianity, and soon started to die out.

Contacts with the New World (because of the high emigration to Latin America due to collapses of local industries), where Cuba had won freedom from Spain in 1898, led to calls for Canarian independence. Most people simply wanted the division of the archipelago into two separate provinces (Las Palmas and Tenerife), which eventually came about in 1927.

Going back in time to the year 1912, the Island Council's Law was brought into force, which led to a number of infrastructure projects such as the airport, reservoirs and the principal motorway network of the island, laying the foundation stone for the development of the tourism industry. Another key date in the history of the Canary Islands is 1982, when the Autonomous Government Statutes were passed.

Government of Gran Canaria

Although under Spanish authority, Gran Canaria has its own government and special status within the EC. King Juan Carlos I and Queen Sofia represent the Spanish monarchy; their son Prince Felipe is heir to the throne.

Even before the Canary Islands were declared a single province of Spain in 1821, competition for primacy between the two main islands (Tenerife and Gran Canaria) had long been intense.

In the new Spanish Constitution of 1978, the Canary Islands were granted autonomous-region status. In practice this means the archipelago is not completely independent from Spain, but that the regional government does enjoy a great deal of freedom with regard to dealings with internal island affairs.

In 1982 the Canary Islands finally saw their dreams of autonomy come true. Santa Cruz de Tenerife (for the western islands) and Las Palmas (for the eastern islands) jointly conduct the government. Las Palmas has half of the regional government departments while the parliament and its governor are elected by the people of the Canary Islands and appointed by Madrid. The parliament, with 60 delegates, always meets in Santa Cruz de Tenerife.

Gran Canaria, as the third largest island, has 15 members in the Canarian Parliament, an organ that, besides its legislative role, sets island budgets and nominates representatives to present Canarian-related affairs to relevant bodies on the mainland.

Each of the Canary Islands has a *cabildo insular* (town hall) which allows them to self-govern to a certain extent and to assume control of local services. The islands are further divided into 77 *municipios* (municipalities), 21 of which can be found in Gran Canaria. An *alcalde* (mayor) heads up each of these Canarian *municipios*.

Economy & Industries

The main bulk of the Canarian economy centres on the tourism industry, accounting for up to 80 per cent of the gross income of the archipelago. With one of the most favourable climates in the world, the Canary Islands attract millions of tourists every year. Besides that, locals rely on the banana industry, other agricultural exports and new tourism-related service industries to make a living.

In the centuries following the Spanish conquest, the mainstays of the Canarian economy were the sugar and winemaking industries. Sugar production on the islands started right after the conquest with sugar-cane imported from Madeira, but it declined in the middle of the 16th century. This was due to the strong competition from Brazil and the Caribbean, which could produce sugar much cheaper. The winemaking industry, which enjoyed its peak during the 16th century, collapsed at the beginning of the 18th century due to a locust plague and mildew attacks, which destroyed the vineyards. However, it has since been revived, with the wines of Gran Canaria, Lanzarote, La Palma and Tenerife proving increasingly popular.

From about 1830 to 1870, as the demand for carmine food dye grew, cochineal production boomed throughout the islands - promising a better future, particularly for the poorer population. Yet this dream did not last very long. The development of synthetic dyes had a considerable impact, causing the decline of the cochineal industry.

However, the archipelago's economy was saved around 1850 with the introduction of the industrial cultivation of bananas to the islands. Growing the fruit gradually gained in importance and bananas became the islands' main export product, reaching its peak at the start of the 20th century. Yet again, there was strong competition surrounding foreign exports, this time from Latin American countries. Surviving on exporting bananas alone was hopeless and local farmers were forced to diversify by cultivating tomatoes, potatoes, other vegetables and exotic fruits.

Today, bananas sold on the Spanish market are protected against foreign suppliers, but their cultivation has become unprofitable due to higher costs and water shortage. Tomatoes are grown on a large scale, mainly for exports between November and April. In recent years the cultivation of flowers and plants for export has also developed into a flourishing industry.

The Environment in

One of the regions with the greatest biodiversity on the planet, Gran Canaria boasts spectacular volcanic landscapes, rare Laurisilva forests, pristine beaches, fertile valleys and transparent waters full of life. Protected natural reserves make up about 40% of the island, with over 100 indigenous species found nowhere else in the world.

UNESCO has granted Gran Canaria the esteemed status of a Biosphere Reserve, in recognition of its biodiversity and to actively support conservation on the island.

Over the past few decades, people living on Gran Canaria have experienced a growing awareness about the environment. The island has few rivers or fresh water sources, so getting clean drinking water is a real issue. Renewable energy sources are also necessary due to the remoteness of the island.

Experts have developed and implemented renewable energy solutions to harness the abundance of sun, wind and sea. Gran Canaria has optimum conditions for producing solar energy, due to the consistently warm climate throughout the year. Solar-powered desalination plants can also transform seawater into clean water for drinking and agricultural use. The largest wind farm in Spain can be found in Arinaga, on the eastern coast of Gran Canaria, and many more are being developed.

Luxury hotels and resorts are beginning to develop responsible environmental policies, while grants have been introduced to promote sustainable resources in local construction, industry and transport. Recycling points have also been installed throughout the island to reduce excessive urban waste.

Visitors are encouraged to do their utmost to respect and conserve the stunning natural environment, as the island continues to make its name as a sustainable holiday destination.

Note:
Some hotels even request your co-operation when it comes to water consumption (for example, you might be asked to put your towels out for washing only when they are dirty instead of doing it daily).

Plant Life in Gran Canaria

The Canary Islands boast almost 2,000 different species of plants, approximately 700 of which are endemic. Many of these species may only be known to flora and fauna enthusiasts, but their beauty, dramatic shapes and rich colours can be observed throughout the island and can be appreciated by everyone.

In mountainous areas at altitudes over 1,000 metres (3,280ft) you will find the Canary Island Pine (Pinus canariensis) which can grow up to 60 metres. It is a large evergreen tree with a resinous bark which allows it to withstand forest fires and live for hundreds of years. Its needles can grow from 15-30 cm (6-12 in) in length. The Canary Island Date Palm (Phoenix canariensis) inhabits shrub lands and semi-desert regions. It is mainly an ornamental plant, although a small amount of edible fruit does grow from it, but not enough to consider eating. One of the most unusual species to be found in the Canaries is the Dragon Tree(Dracaena draco). This tree grows very slowly and can have either a single or multiple trunk growing up to 12 metres tall with dense leaves that form a kind of umbrella shape at the top. It takes about ten years for the tree to reach just one metre tall. There are many fine specimens of this tree to be found in the Canary Islands, including the renowned Dragon Tree in Tenerife which is an ancient specimen located in Icod de los Vinos in the north of the island. This particular tree is believed to be more than one thousand years old.

One of the most common inhabitants of the laurel forests is the Canary Holly (Ilex canariensis), an evergreen tree also known as Small-Leaf Holly. The bark of this tree is said to have medicinal properties. The Canary Island Wallflower (Erysimum scoparium), a woody, endemic shrub with pink-mauve flowers, grows in the highest regions of the islands.

Another native plant to be found is the Canary Island Spurge (Euphorbia canariensis), a cactus-like tree, with spindly arms and reddish-green flowers. The white Tajinaste (Echium decaisnei), an endemic variety of borage, with sword-shaped leaves and tiny white flowers, also thrives in dry, rocky areas. The coastal basalt rocks are often covered by another distinctive native species, the fleshy Canary Samphire (Astydamia latifolia), which flowers in early spring, while the decorative Balsamic Spurge (Euphorbia Balsamifera) is mainly to be found in semi-desert areas.

These are just a few examples we have picked out from an abundance of native plants that are found growing in the microclimates of the island. In addition to the endemic species, you will find countless imported species from all corners of the world in the Jardín Botánico Viera y Clavijo (in Tafira near the city of Las Palmas) and Cactualdea (a cacti park in San Nicolás de Tolentino). You will find more information on Jardín Botánico and Cactualdea in our guide by clicking on 'Things to Do', then 'Fun and Theme Parks'. By touring the island at your leisure you'll see a wide variety of colourful, exotic plants in all their beauty growing wild in their natural surroundings.

Tourism

From the second half of the 19th century, Gran Canaria started gaining popularity in European circles as an attractive base for recreational holidays; a place for people in need of a rest. Shipping companies soon took advantage of this development and equipped their vessels with cabins for the transport of passengers. These companies would go on to build the first hotels on the island, one of which was the Hotel Santa Catalina (1890) in Las Palmas de Gran Canaria. This is the only hotel dating from the early beginnings of tourism that still remains open.

In 1912 the Island Council Law was brought into force and the foundation stone for the development of the tourism industry and its related services was laid. This led to a number of infrastructure projects such as the construction of the airport, water reservoirs and the principal motorway network of the island. During the first half of the 20th century a number of wars (World Wars I and II and the Spanish Civil War) impeded further growth. Not even the opening of the then-called Gando Airport (Gran Canaria's first airport) in 1930 could spark a new boost to the tourism industry. It was only in 1957 when an aircraft from the Swedish airline TSA landed on the island with all of its 54 seats completely booked that tourism really starting taking off. This was the first of many charter flights to arrive on the island from that date on.

Eventually, building on the boom of the 1960s, tourism became the main source of income for the island, making Gran Canaria one of the most sought-after tourist destinations in the world.

Today tourism in Gran Canaria is mainly about beaches, water sports, nightlife and leisure parks, especially when it comes to the south of the island. This is the place, where you find water and theme parks, shopping malls, discos, and many hours of sun. Tourists coming to the southern sandy beaches and dunes have brought more wealth to Gran Canaria than banana plantations could ever have done tourism has grown from less than a hundred visitors a year at the end of the 19th century to 11 million visitors per year in the beginning of the new millennium.

The north of the island is more orientated to the business visitor, hosting all sorts of facilities for the organisation of conferences, seminars and business meetings. This is also the area where you'll find the cosmopolitan city of Las Palmas, the island's business centre, and the busy port Puerto de la Luz, one of Europe's most important harbours. The sandy beaches of Las Canteras and Las Alcaravaneras, flanking the city of Las Palmas, account for a stable income from tourism in this north-eastern area.

And if you want to get away from it all, Gran Canaria provides the perfect destination for a holiday. It's not difficult to get off the beaten track when there are over 300km of footpaths. Rural tourism has become increasingly popular with the renovation and improvement of facilities available at casas rurales (rural houses). These include cave houses where you can get as close to nature as is humanly possible.

Note:
Gran Canaria is also attracting more and more visitors with niche markets, which have emerged in the past years, such as golf or wellness holidays or rural tourism, adding even more attractions to this already eclectic destination and making it one of the most accomplished in Europe

The People and Culture

Culturally speaking, Gran Canaria is synonymous with the blending of cultures. This attribute of the island is the legacy of its long history as a port of call for travellers, having been a society that is open to everything that arrives to its shores from beyond the seas.

The march of time through the islands has left behind an extremely valuable archaeological, artistic, architectural and ethnographic heritage, which bears witness to the cultural evolvement of our island community. This historic heritage, the legacy of the island's own identity, has been enriched and accompanied by multifarious manifestations of art and culture, which has endowed the island with certain unique traits that would be difficult to find in any other territory of such a limited extent.

Most of the monuments that can be seen in Gran Canaria date from after the period of conquest, although certain archaeological sites and areas relating to the early inhabitants of the islands have been successfully preserved (such as the painted caves named Cuevas Pintadas de Gáldar and the Cenobio or convent de Valerón).

In addition to the archaeological and artistic manifestations that date from the various early and contemporary moments in the history of this island, which are spread out across the entire length and breadth of the island, Gran Canaria also boasts a broad and varied calendar of cultural activities that take place throughout the year. Even the most discerning public will be delighted by the current cultural life of the islands, which includes concerts, international music and cinema festivals, exhibitions and conference cycles that feature speakers of international renown. One such cultural event that deserves special mention is the internationally famed Canary Islands Music Festival, which takes place at the start of each year, this being the only music festival in the whole of Europe that is held in winter. Practically all the main figures in the music world have participated in this festival, this being the arena for many a debut.

Gastronomy

The climate of Gran Canaria, the way of its people and even the way of speaking is mellow, for which reason it is not surprising that the fruit of its land and many of the products produced in Gran Canaria are also sweet. Even Shakespeare in his plays longingly sighed for the wine of this land, the "Malvasía", which is of course sweet.

Lose yourself in our fertile lowlands in the search for exotic mangos, papayas (or paw paws) and bananas; discover the natural water springs, and don't forget to flavour the gastronomy of each village and their typical deserts, elaborated for centuries with excellent raw materials (meat, fish, fruit and vegetables) with original and tasty recipes.

A brief taster of some traditional Gran Canarian dishes begins with the "Enyesques" (aperitifs), where we find the famous "Papas Arrugadas" (small jacket potatoes in traditional Canarian "mojo" sauce), "Ropa Vieja" (a meat and chickpea stew) or Carajacas (fried filleted liver in a spicy marinated sauce); followed by first plate dishes, such as the "Caldo de pescado" (fish soup) or "Potaje de Berros" (watercress potage) and second plate dishes, that can comprise meat dishes, such as "Conejo en Salmorejo" (Samorejo Rabbit) or fish dishes, such as Vieja Sancochada (Parboiled Vieja).

To finish off we can sweeten our palate with any of the desserts, such as Bienmesabe (a dessert made from egg yolk, sugar and almonds) or Huevos Mole (sweet whipped egg yolk).

"Canarians are like the Giant Teide, snowy quietness on the outside and fire in the heart..." (folk song).

Long before the first European sailors arrived on the Canary Islands, all seven islands were inhabited. Guanches, 'guan' (meaning 'man') and 'che' (meaning 'white mountain', referring to the snow-crowned Teide on Tenerife) in the native tongue, was the general name given to those inhabitants, although in fact all the islands have their own unique aboriginal names. For example, the people of Gran Canaria are known as Canarios. Guanches are believed to have arrived on the islands between the 5th and the 1st century B.C., probably from Africa. According to Spanish historical records, the Guanches were tall, strongly built, white-skinned, blue-eyed and blond-haired.

The Guanches were cave dwellers, which was a logical development with regard to the climate of the Canary Islands. A cave dwelling was the perfect solution for both summer and winter, keeping people cooler or warmer, and also ideal for storage purposes.

But how did the Guanches arrive on the islands if there's no evidence of Guanche boats? Actually, no one knows for sure, although people think that pirates marooned them there or they could have been convicts exiled by Romans or Carthaginians. Another theory says that they may have floated across from North Africa on reed craft.

Although the Guanches learned how to adjust their way of life to the rocky landscapes and lived in caves or simple huts built out of rocks, their society was not entirely primitive: they had a relatively sophisticated social structure. This varied from island to island, but most of them had a tribal structure, ruled by a chieftain who was in turn advised by a council of elders. When discovered by the Spaniards, the natives were advanced enough to use pottery. Their main foods were milk, butter, goat and pork, and some fruits. Their clothing consisted of leather tunics or vests made of plaited rushes. They left alphabet-like characters and rock carvings and paintings, yet the meanings of these remain obscure.

Today, Gran Canaria boasts an average of 517 people per square kilometre, the highest housing density in the archipelago and in the whole of Europe. Almost half of its population resides in the city of Las Palmas, a place with a great ethnic mix and strong cosmopolitan image.

The inhabitants of Gran Canaria are a proud, friendly and easygoing people, the majority of them being descendants of the Spanish conquerors, colonisers and assimilated Guanches. In general, they are open-minded, willing to help and happy to show visitors their culture and their island.

As a result of having been a bridge between Europe and the continents of America and Africa for so long, many members of other nations in particular merchant families and seafaring people have settled on the Canary Islands from early on. Their descendants are fully integrated in the island's society, where nobody would deny them their status of genuine Canarios.

Almost 96 per cent of the inhabitants of the Canary Islands are very tradition-conscious Roman Catholics, which can be witnessed on big religious feast days and particularly during Semana Santa (Holy Week), when extensive celebrations take place all over the islands

Customs and Traditions

The Canary Islands have rich customs and traditions many of which involve a good party! Carnivals or fiestas are held throughout the year and almost each town has its own celebration. They are vibrant, energetic and are a good way for visitors to learn about the history and culture of Gran Canaria.

During fiestas, the locals dress up in colourful costumes, stalls sell handmade crafts, there are lots of fun games to keep the children amused and of course the food and drink is flowing.

The main carnival is held every year between January and February in Las Palmas. It starts with street parties, known as *verbenas del mogollón*, where thousands of people dress up and dance their way through the streets until the early hours. Another highlight is known as the *murgas*. These are large groups of people who dress up, perform and sing about their discontent and criticisms of the local, regional or national social situation. They often use traditional well-known songs and change the lyrics to express their feelings in a humorous and ironic way.

The main events of the carnival include the gala for choosing the carnival queen and the great carnival parade, which marches through the whole city of Las Palmas.

Another important tradition on the island is the *Romería*. Every year Gran Canaria hosts many *Romerías*, which are religious pilgrimages in honour of a saint. People dress in traditional attire and walk through their town or village accompanied by singing and a band playing musical instruments.

Lucha Canaria, Canarian wrestling, is an ancient custom which dates back to the late 1400s during the times of the first known inhabitants of the islands, the Guanches. Its popularity has grown over the centuries and today it is a major sport covered by Canarian television.

Tour, Travel Tourism: Vacation, Holiday, Honeymoon

Discover Gran Canaria

A veritable continent in miniature, Gran Canaria seduces from the moment you set foot on it.

The summits of Gran Canaria know what snow is, although just a few kilometres away the sun shines all year on golden beaches - and on lakes where you can practice water sports, find freshwater fish, bathe or camp in the great outdoors.

You can tour the island from coast to summit by using the well-maintained roads. But recently the dirt roads have been renovated. In the past, these were used by Canarians to travel on foot or on horseback. Today, they allow visitors and locals alike to discover the places hidden to the eyes of those who travel in a car.

In the capital, Las Palmas de Gran Canaria, you can sun yourself on the beach of Las Canteras, try out all kinds of water sports from sailing to water skiing, and enjoy the numerous gastronomic delights and the intense nightlife. Besides that, you can visit the Canarian Museum, Museo Canario, (exhibiting archaeological remains of the island), the Atlantic Centre of Modern Art, Centro Atlántico de Arte Moderno, or the House of Colombus, Casa de Colón (which ensures the memory of the Admiral lives on). And, just a few kilometres away from Las Palmas de Gran Canaria, travelling towards the centre of the island, in Tafira, you'll find the oldest golf club in the whole of Spain.

! Welcome to Gran Canaria Holiday Guide

Gran Canaria is certainly one of the last remaining European paradise isles located in the Atlantic Ocean, 130 miles from the African coast. It's the third largest of the Canary Islands and has Fuerteventura and Tenerife as its neighbours. Las Palmas, located in the northeast part of the island, is its capital.

Gran Canaria is an island of contrasts. As the most dynamic capital city in the Canaries, it has a great mix of people and keeps local traditions alive, but always catering for the holidaymaker. Crammed with culture, incredibly beautiful coastlines and spectacular beaches with a sunny climate, Gran Canaria is a great destination all year round. So whenever you want to escape for a break, the delights of Canary Islands are waiting for you! And it's all just a mouse-click away... virtually!

From the cooler north to the sunnier south, this perfect holiday island has everything the most discerning traveller could wish for: the great diversity of climate, lush forests, exotic flora and fauna, volcanic craters, the odd flurry of snow on the highest peaks all this has led to this island being dubbed "The Miniature Continent". Where else can you find acres of sand dunes against a backdrop of verdant mountains within easy reach of some of the best hotels, apartments, resorts, clubs, bars and cafés in Europe?

The beautiful island of Gran Canaria has a lot to offer the tourist and a wealth of places to visit. From the north to the south, east to west, it's all here for you to discover. Whether you are with your loved one, in a group of friends or on a family holiday, you are sure to find what you're looking for to make your holiday experience memorable and exciting, not to mention relaxing.

The south is the most popular part of the island, containing such delights as Puerto Mogán (a picturesque village also known as Little Venice), Puerto Rico, Maspalomas, Meloneras, San Agustín and the famous Playa del Inglés. But with such spectacular views and landscapes, make sure you don't miss the rugged north and west coasts, as well as the island's interior.

Meloneras really has the Wow factor. The whole area has been renovated with such style and sophistication, that it became a very classy place. You can walk along the promenade, shop until you drop in high-end designer stores like Lacoste and Ralph Laurenbefore sampling cuisine from a whole host of restaurants, including Italian, traditional Spanish tapas, sushi and seafood.

Dip a toe in the warm waters at Playa del Inglés and top up your tan on the beach there. It's full of great places to eat and drink, giving you a perfect place to rest and recharge your batteries. By night, Playa del Inglés really comes alive. If you like music and dancing, this is the place to go!

The sand dunes of Maspalomas are a sight to behold, stretching out along the south coast and looking like giant waves of sand covering around 4 square kilometres.

Picturesque Puerto de Mogán is a very popular destination and it's easy to understand why with its canal-like channels and quaint bridges, it is also known as Little Venice.

And of course the vibrant capital, Las Palmas is crammed with culture and history. This is a truly cosmopolitan city located on the northeastern part of the island with so much to do and see museums, art collections, fantastic architecture, beautiful parks, great **shops**, cafés and also the famous Las Canteras Beach, perfect for a cooling dip or as a spot of sunbathing.

Enjoying warm weather all year round, our island offers you a wealth of choices. Not only will you find the exact locations of hotels, great offers and unbeatable prices on this website, you will also find all the information you need to plan and book your holiday in Gran Canaria an in-depth guide to the most interesting places to see, the most popular beaches, car hire, hotels and resorts, weather, getting around and all those essential travel tips that are usually so hard to find.

Essential Information
You'll find all the information you need to plan and prepare for your holiday as well as plenty of related material.

Places To See
We show you all the best places to visit. Whatever your taste, you'll find something that interests you!

Weather And Climate

Check out the current weather, temperature forecasts, satellite images and the annual averages.

Where To Stay

Whatever you are looking for in your holiday, Spain Gran Canaria has the answers.

Do you want to stay at the best hotels the island has to offer? Of course you do...

spain-grancanaria.com gives you the best the best holiday experience, the best locations, the best prices and the best hotels. We have specially chosen a selection of 4 and 5-star luxury hotels, including apartments, villas, resorts and hostels all over the island. So depending on where you would like to stay, we can guarantee you quality accommodation with the promise that you will not be disappointed. All of our hotels have been carefully selected and cater for all types of holidaymakers, from courting couples to families or lone travellers to large groups of friends. We also have a range of car rentals if you fancy getting behind the wheel and touring the island in the sunshine.

This fascinating island has something for everyone. Whatever your taste or age, you will find the perfect location to spend your precious time and a huge variety of things to do to transform your trip into the holiday of a lifetime.

Gran Canaria, the Children's Choice...

Gran Canaria is a perfect destination for families, with a wide variety of activities for youngsters in addition to enjoying the natural splendours that the island proudly boasts, 365 days a year.

The Island's own natural amenities are one of the main attractions for children. The amazing abundance of nature, with its numerous, breath taking, good quality beaches and the temperate climate, all combine to give the sea a pleasant swimming temperature of approximately 20 degrees in the winter months and 24 degrees for the remaining months guaranteeing all year round open air fun!

The Island has many sheltered, safe swimming beaches equipped with children's play areas to keep the little ones happy. The majority of the hotels and extra-hotel complexes in Gran Canaria also have babysitting services with specialised staff or specific activities to entertain children keeping them occupied whilst you enjoy the sun, catch up on some rest and relaxation or slip off to explore the many natural attractions.

"Bungalows" offer another advantage to families travelling with children as they provide one or two bedrooms with a living room, kitchen, bathroom and pretty private gardens. This gives families space to enjoy their holidays in comfort and often include all the services of a hotel.

Natural resources also play an important part in the facilities on offer for children. The Island has various parks, entertainment complexes and nature interpretation centres offering an alternative for children to learn and have fun at the same time.

It's Just One Great Theme Park

Gran Canaria offers a wide range of leisure activities providing fun for all the family. These include theme parks, tourist trips, land and sea excursions.

There are a wide variety of natural theme parks offering different experiences such as Cactualdea (San Nicolás de Tolentino) which is a botanical park with a great selection of cactus, palm trees and tropical plants or why not visit Palmitos Park (San Bartolomé de Tirajana) which again is an exotic garden combining birds and orchids or the Parque Los Cocodrilos / Crocodile Park (Agüimes) which specialises in alligators, crocodiles and other types of reptiles! For all those cowboy and Indian fans, why not visit Sioux City (San Bartolomé de Tirajana) which covers 320,000 square metres and looks just like a North

American western town, with its houses, churches, ranch, bank, saloons where "wild west" scenarios are recreated!

For families who would like to discover the least exploited and remotest spots of Gran Canaria, you can choose to walk and explore the different royal paths of centuries-old tracks that were once the only way of getting around the Island. Alternatively for those who want to have a more exotic experience, you can take an excursion on the back of a dromedary through the famous Maspalomas Dunes or along the Fataga valley. For those interested in a bit of underwater fun, what better way to view the seabeds than taking a trip along the coast in a glass bottomed boat and if you are lucky experience the thrill of seeing the Dolphins and Whales swim and dive alongside!

Finally, for other exciting water fun theme parks Gran Canaria has four, namely 'Aquapark', 'Aquasur', 'Oceanpark' and 'The Holiday World' fun park. The children will love these so why not visit them all! Gran Canaria has it all ensuring a family holiday filled with fond memories of an exilerating, action packed and diverse holiday that will leave you wanting to come back again and again.

Tourism Information Offices

There are many tourist offices ('Oficinas de turismo'), kiosks and points spread all over the island providing tourists with information on any matters related to the island's culture, events, places of interest and anything you can think of.

Airport
Llegadas Comunitarias - Puerta A. Aeropuerto de Gran Canaria
+34 928 574 117

Las Palmas de Gran Canaria
Calle León y Castillo 17
+34 928 219 600

Pueblo Canario
Plaza de Las Palmeras 3
+34 928 243 593

Plaza de Hurtado Mendoza
Plaza de las Ranas
+34 928 446 824

Parque de San Telmo
+34 928 446 824

Paseo de la Playa de Las Canteras (in front of the Hotel Cristina Las Palmas)
+34 928 446 824

Avenida José Mesa y López (between the two Corte Inglés department stores)

Mogán
Avenida de Mogán
+34 928 158 804

Moya
Calle Juan Delgado (Parque Pico Lomito) 6
+34 928 612 348

Playa del Inglés
Avenida España, corner of Avenida EE.UU (Centro Comercial Yumbo)
+34 928 771 550

Paseo Maritimo
Centro Comercial Anexo II Local 20
+34 928 768 409

Avenida de Tirajana 1 (below the Riu Palace Maspalomas hotel)
+34 928 765 242

San Mateo
Calle Doctor Ramírez Cabrera 9
+34 928 661 350 extension 45

Santa Brígida

Gran Canaria

+34 928 446 824

Parque de Santa Catalina
+34 928 446 824

Agaete
Calle Nuestra Señora de las Nieves 1
+34 928 554 382

Agüimes
Plaza de San Antón
+34 928 124 183

Artenara
Calle Párroco Domingo Báez 13
+34 928 666 102

Arucas
Plaza de la Constitución 2
+34 928 623 136

Firgas
Calle El Molino 12
+34 928 616 747

Gáldar
Calle Plaza de Santiago 1
+34 928 895 855

Ingenio
Calle Pascual Richart (Casa de Postas) 2
+34 928 783 799

La Aldea de San Nicolás
Calle 18 de Julio 5
+34 928 641 059

Santa Lucía de Tirajana
Avenida de Canarias - Plaza de la Era, Vecindario
+34 928 125 260

Santa María de Guía de Gran Canaria
Calle San José
+34 928 553 043

Tejeda
Calle Leocadio Cabrera
+34 928 666 189

Telde
Calle León y Castillo 2
+34 928 013 331

Teror
Casa Huerta 1
+34 928 613 808

Tunte
Calle Reyes Católicos, San Bartolomé de Tirajana
+34 928 127 378

Valleseco
Calle León y Castillo 27
+34 928 618 740

Calle Doctor Fleming 57

+34 928 890 378

Maspalomas Mirador del Golf

Avenida Turoperador Tui (Campo Internacional)

+34 928 769 585

Valsequillo

Calle León y Castillo 2

+34 928 705 011 extension 0411

What to See

Places to see in Gran Canaria

There is so much of interest to see in Gran Canaria that you will undoubtedly find you don't have sufficient time to visit all the places you'd like to. So to really see and appreciate what Gran Canaria has to offer, here's a quick glance at the must-see of the island:

The City of Las Palmas:

Places to visit: Vegueta - Triana - Ciudad Jardín - Santa Catalina - Playa de las Canteras - La Isleta

Gran Canaria's North:

When exploring the north of the island - and you want to make the most of it there are two specific and different areas, the inland and the coast.

Inland

Places to visit: Arucas Firgas Moya Valleseco Teror

Coast

Places to visit: Santa María de Guía Gáldar Agaete Puerto de las Nieves

East to South of Gran Canaria:

Places to visit: Telde Valsequillo Ingenio Agüimes Barranco de Guayadeque Santa Lucía de Tirajana San Bartolomé de Tirajana Fataga

South to West of Gran Canaria:

Places to visit: Meloneras - Maspalomas Dunes Playa del Inglés Pasito Blanco Arguineguín Puerto Rico Puerto Mogán Mogán San Nicolás de Tolentino Puerto de la Aldea

The Centre of the Island:

Places to visit: Tafira Jardín Botánico Canario Viera y Clavijo Caldera de Bandama Santa Brígida Vega de San Mateo Pico de las Nieves - Tejeda Artenara

Top beaches of Gran Canaria:

Beaches to visit: Playa de las Canteras Playa de las Alcaravaneras San Agustín Playa del Inglés Maspalomas Playa de Puerto Rico Playa de los Amadores Puerto Mogán Playa Meloneras

Most people understand a tourist's unfamiliarity with the terrain when navigating the island and you'll find the majority of Canarian drivers friendly and courteous. Petrol stations are dotted throughout the island - but do fill up before leaving on a major excursion. Stay within the legal speed limits and remember that drinking alcohol and driving is an offence throughout Europe. Belt up, take it easy and enjoy the beauty of Gran Canaria.

North Coastal and Inland

There's so much of interest to see in Gran Canaria that you will be spoilt for choice! The travel experts from Spain-Grancanaria have condensed the major attractions into easy-to-follow guides that help you get the best out of your holiday.

Starting on the northeast coast, the capital city of Gran Canaria, Las Palmas, is a mandatory stop. Vegueta, one of the oldest quarters in the city, has charming squares, such as Plaza Santa Ana, and the impressive Catedral de Santa Ana. In Triana, a much more bourgeoisie district, you'll be surrounded by buildings dating back to the 18th, 19th and 20th centuries, all lined up along Calle Triana, a whole street declared national historic monument.

If you are travelling around the northern coastal areas there are some charming pretty little villages and towns to look out for. Santa María de Guía is full of Canarian character, history and is an enchanting place to visit. Just as captivating is the fishing village of Puerto de las Nieves; here you will find the lovely little chapel Ermita de las Nieves and the breathtaking natural rock formation Dedo de Dios (God's finger). The lovely town of Agaete is more than 500 years old and is surrounded by steep slopes packed with colourful vegetation — fantastic for photographs.

For a lively atmosphere, attractive plazas, shopping, culture and all the hustle and bustle of a vibrant town, check out Gáldar, which is also steeped in Guanche history.

Moving further away from the coast towards the island's inland, the mountains become more evident, and you may visit several towns with many historical monuments, such as Arucas' huge neo-Gothic cathedral or Teror's colonial-style buildings.

The roads are quite narrow, bendy and steep in this area so buckle up and enjoy the fantastic panoramic views that will unfold around every corner!

City of Las Palmas

Las Palmas de Gran Canaria, the capital of the island, is located in the north-eastern part of the island set in magnificent scenery composed of two bays and their beautiful beaches Playa de las Canteras and Playa de las Alcaravaneras.

Founded in 1478, Las Palmas de Gran Canaria boasts an important historical and cultural heritage, much of which can be found in the district of Vegueta, the oldest quarter of the town, which was declared a UNESCO World Heritage Site in 1990.

Originating from a Castillian military encampment on the right hillside of the ravine Barranco de Guiniguada where the San Antonio Abad chapel is located today the first settlement, named Real de Las Palmas, expanded towards the banks of the ravine developing into the quarters of Vegueta and Triana on the right and left bank of the Barranco de Guiniguada. Today, Las Palmas' major highway, Calle Juan de Quesada, which crosses the Barranco de Guiniguada and leads out of town to the centre of the island, separates these two historic quarters.

For almost 400 years the city was limited to the north within the perimeter of the walled quarters of Vegueta and Triana and during the 16th, 17th and 18th centuries the town grew primarily into the interior of the island as almost all the cities of the archipelago.

Vegueta, Triana, San José and some small neighbourhoods inhabited by immigrants and fishermen mainly constituted the city of Las Palmas. Only in the 19th century benefiting from the construction of the port Puerto de la Luz the city start expanding to the north along the coastal strip and the districts of Arenales, Ciudad Jardín, Alcaravaneras, Santa Catalina and La Isleta emerged.

Las Palmas de Gran Canaria has an impressive infrastructure of hotels and apartments and its harbour Puerto de La Luz is one of the most important in all Europe, giving the city a very cosmopolitan image. Only under the impulse of tourism and economic activities of the 60s was the city finally consolidated and settled with a population that has doubled in the last 30 years (actually around 400,000 inhabitants).

Today, Las Palmas de Gran Canaria is a bustling city overflowing with Spanish ambience, history and culture. Lucha canaria (Canarian wrestling) and vela latina (Canarian lateen sailing) are native sports originating in the capital of Gran Canaria. Indeed, almost every weekend you can observe vela latina regattas going out to the sea.

Vegueta

The most interesting sights to see: Only a few metres away from the site of the military encampment, from which the first settlement originated, you will find the Plaza Santa Ana with its entrance guarded by bronze statues of dogs symbolising the legendary canine, which since 1506 was said to have appeared in the town's heights, and some impressive historic buildings, of which many have survived in their original state up to date.

Noteworthy among these magnificent buildings are the Casa Regental, a largely 17th-century building serving as residence of the president of Gran Canaria's High Court of Law, the elegant 19th-century building of the Casas Consistoriales (Town Hall) and the Palacio Episcopal (Bishop's Palace), of which only an ornate single-storey façade remained after the great fire of 1599, and the imposing Catedral de Santa Ana.

Staying in the Vegueta district, on Calle del Doctor Chil, you'll find the Church of the old Augustinian Convent, where the High Court sits today, the baroque Church of San Francisco de Asís, the sombre-looking Old Seminary and, last but not least, the Museo Canario (Canary Island Museum) at the corner of Calle Doctor Verneau.

Just around the corner from the Museo Canario is the Plaza del Espíritu Santo (Square of the Holy Spirit), a charming square with an impressive monumental fountain located in its centre, surrounded by a number of stately historical houses and the Chapel of the Holy Spirit. This is well worth a visit.

Santa Ana Cathedral

At the heart of the Vegueta quarter sits the twin-towered Santa Ana Cathedral, the first church in the Canaries, which was built on the orders of *Los Reyes Católicos*, Queen Isabella I of Castile and King Ferdinand II of Aragon, after Gran Canaria was conquered in 1478.

Construction started around 1500 and was not completed until almost four centuries later, making the intervention of several architects and artists inevitable, the result of which can be seen in three basic architectural styles: Gothic, Renaissance and Neoclassical.

Very little is known of the original plans but, according to some existing drawings, the works began as a Gothic structure with three naves of the same height. Some remarkable pieces of art can still be seen in the chapels of the cathedral including many statues, most of which are from the famous religious sculptor José Luján Pérez.

In the south wing of the cathedral, the *Patio de los Naranjos* (Patio of Orange trees), you'll find the *Museo Diocesano de Arte Sacro* (Sacred Art Museum) exhibiting many valuable sacred artefacts, some noteworthy paintings, including works by Dutch masters, and a collection of Spanish sculptures, gathered from the last four centuries.

Triana

The district of Triana, together with Vegueta one of the oldest districts of the city, has turned into Las Palmas' main commercial centre especially since its main street became a pedestrianized zone with a multitude of retail outlets, ranging from tiny old-fashioned shops to big chain stores and up-market boutiques.

In contrast to the Vegueta quarter, which because of its narrow streets and older buildings transports you to the Middle Ages, the Triana quarter is far more bourgeoisie as mainly local, Andalusian, English, Maltese and Danish merchant families settled in this area. This also explains why the main street which crosses the whole district displays the fashionable architectural styles of the 18th, 19th and 20th century. In spite of a stretch of modern houses at the beginning of the Calle Triana, the entire street was declared a national historic monument.

In the south of Triana, almost opposite the *Mercado de Vegueta*, you'll find the *Teatro Pérez Galdós*, named after Spain's second most famous writer after Cervantes. No longer neglected from the outside following a stunning face-lift, the venue features opulent interior decorations and a spacious auditorium. Offering a diverse programme, visit Pérez Galdós for classical recitals, jazz concerts, plays and more. Nearby, at the corner of Calle Cano/Calle Peregrina streets stands the Casa Museo de Pérez Galdós.

Continuing through Triana, close to the Casa Museo Pérez Galdós, you will come across a charming little square, the Plaza de Cairasco, at the northern end of which the splendidly art-nouveau Gabinete Literario is located, a building that originally opened in 1844 now houses a literary society as well as a restaurant/café with a nice, shady terrace. Another place of interest to be found in this corner of the city, where much of its cultural life takes place, is the grand building of the Centro Cultural de La Caja de Canarias (commonly known as CICCA), a small-but-perfectly-formed venue.

To the side of this small square runs the Alameda de Colón, where at the northern end, near a bust of Columbus, you will find the whitewashed, colonial-style Iglesia de San Francisco de Asís, which has three naves, a white marble floor, the typical Mudéjar ceiling and some important works by noted Canarian religious sculptor, José Luján Pérez. Destroyed by a fire in 1599 caused by an attack by Dutch pirates, this church was rebuilt during the 17th century and then became a parochial church when the monks were ejected (as they were throughout Spain in 1821).

Note:

In the north of the Triana district lays arguably Las Palmas' most picturesque park, *Parque San Telmo*, which can't be missed, as it's here where you'll find the city's main underground bus station and a major taxi rank. With shady palm trees, benches, a children' s playground and a bandstand, San Telmo provides respite from the hustle and bustle of Triana. Other attractions include a magnificent art-deco café, splendidly decorated with multi-coloured gleaming tiles, where you can enjoy a cold drink and/or snack under towering trees, and the small late-Baroque *Ermita de San Telmo chapel*, dedicated to sailors and fisherman. Nearby is the *Gobierno Militar* (Armed-Forces Headquarters) where General Franco launched the Spanish Civil War in 1936, a plaque marking the spot where he announced his rebellion.

Ciudad Jardín

A true oasis in the bustling city of Las Palmas, Ciudad Jardín was established by British residents who dominated the economic life of the region during the late 19th century. In this part of town, you will find many embassies and elegant residential houses set in small gardens, displaying various architectural styles.

The main feature of this district is the large Parque Doramas, a beautifully- landscaped park with water features, interesting statues, a municipal swimming pool and numerous examples of endemic flowers and plants. A monument depicting aboriginal people tumbling over a precipice to escape capture, symbolises resistance of the Guanche chief Doramas, after whom this park was named. On Sundays it's a popular destination for families as there's a free show, typically clowns or puppets.

Amid the lush sub-tropical greenery of this park stands the grand Hotel Santa Catalina, which was originally built in 1890 and most recently renovated in 2005. Many celebrities and members of royalty such as Winston Churchill, Agatha Christie and Prince Charles have stayed in this outstanding hotel but visitors can also enjoy the beautiful views of the park from its bar. We thoroughly recommend staying at this luxurious 5-star establishment, which you will find in the hotel pages of our guide. There are also alternative options in other areas of the city including AC Hotel Gan Canaria and Hotel Cristina Las Palmas.

Also enclosed in the Parque Doramas are the Pueblo Canario (Canarian Village) and the Museo Néstor.

Opposite the Parque Doramas area you will find some of the city's important water sports centres including the Club Natación Metropole, a swimming and sports club. An underpass leads below

Avenida Marítima to the *Muelle Deportivo*, the yacht harbour, which has a new seaside promenade. There are also bars, restaurants and a nightclub, making this a pleasant area to relax and soak up the atmosphere.

Adjoining the harbour is Playa de las Alcaravaneras, a 550 metre stretch of golden sand frequented mainly by locals, flanked in the south by the Varadero Sailing Club and to the north by the chic Real Club Náutico (Royal Sailing Club), where you're always guaranteed to spot some glamorous ocean-going yachts.

Santa Catalina

Between the harbour Puerto de la Luz in the east and the Playa de las Canteras to the west, you'll find the bustling district of Santa Catalina, where, especially along the Calle Mesa y López boulevard, most of the big stores can be found, including two branches of Spain's largest department store El Corte Inglés, as well as specialised shops and elegant boutiques. The heart of this district is the big and busy *Parque Santa Catalina* which is actually more of a square dotted with palm trees and flowerbeds than a park where a sizeable slice of Las Palmas' nightlife takes place. Numerous restaurants, bars, clubs and discos attract fun-loving locals and visitors until dawn.

But also during daytime there is always a lot of activity here, with people doing their shopping or frequenting the many outdoor cafés, crowds of elderly men playing cards, chess and dominos and tourists getting information at the tourist information point. It's also where the city's sightseeing bus (guagua turística) begins its tour. At carnival time a big stage is erected here and the *Parque Santa Catalina* becomes the centre of the city's colourful and exciting celebrations. A role it repeats during the popular WOMAD music festival in November.

On the port side of the park you will find the outstanding *Museo Elder de la Ciencia y la Tecnología*, an impressive and well-organised science and technology museum, accommodated in a building that formerly belonged to the Elder-Dempster Shipping Line, hence the name. In this museum, motto: forbidden not to touch, visitors especially children can entertain themselves for hours on end.

A landscaped pedestrianised area leads from the museum to the *Muelle Santa Catalina*, the ferry terminal for connections to Tenerife and other Canarian islands, located at the south side of the Avenida Marítima.

Overlooking Parque Santa Catalina is the AC Hotel Gran Canaria, a perfect base from which to explore the riches of this city. Enjoy 4-star luxury, sophisticated accommodation and a wealth of facilities, located in the heart of this exciting capital. Spain-Grancanaria only works with the best hotels on the island and this surely is one of them.

Note:
In front of the ferry terminal you will find an entrance to the city's second underground bus station and to the left of it, overlooking the port, there is the ultra-stylish shopping centre El Muelle gleaming in shades of blue and yellow with numerous big-name chain stores, cinemas, discos, open-air restaurants and cafés.

Playa de las Canteras

Bordered to the east by Santa Catalina and to the north by La Isleta, you'll find the district of Playa de las Canteras, Gran Canaria's very first tourist resort. Here you'll find lots of hotels, offices, shops, restaurants, bars and... one of Spain's best urban beaches the Playa de las Canteras from which this district takes its name.

And close to this fine stretch of beach we have a handful of hotels perfectly placed so you will not have to travel too far to chill out on the sand and enjoy the sea.

Overlooking the beautiful ocean, two hotels, AC Hotel Gran Canaria and Hotel Cristina Las Palmas, both come with an endorsement from

Spain-Grancanaria and are the perfect setting for a holiday in this cosmopolitan city. Or, join the exclusive guest list at the magnificent Hotel Santa Catalina, a stunning building set slightly further inland. A complimentary shuttle service runs daily to the beach.

At the southern end of Playa de las Canteras, a formerly quite neglected area, a landscaped promenade leads to the Auditorio Alfredo Kraus, a masterpiece of modern architecture and home to the Las Palmas Philharmonic Orchestra.

Built in 1997 as a tribute to the famous Canarian tenor Alfredo Kraus, this building, which also incorporates the Canary Islands Convention Centre, was designed by Catalan architect, Óscar Tusquets, and Canarian sculptor, Juan Bordes.

Constructed in solid natural stone, the Auditorio boasts, in total, ten concert halls (one big concert hall and nine smaller ones) serves as a venue for operas and concerts, as well as the Las Palmas de Gran Canaria International Film Festival and the Canary Islands Classical Music Festival.

Note:
This area also boasts the city's biggest shopping centre, Las Arenas, with a wide range of shops, a mouth-watering selection of restaurants and snack bars, as well as a multi-screen cinema.

La Isleta

From the northern end of the district of Playa de las Canteras, you're within walking distance of the old fishermen's quarter of La Isleta, situated on a small peninsula.

Built on steep terrain, La Isleta features narrow streets with many street vendors, old small shops, bars and an important Spanish naval base. The centre of this district forms the Plaza Ingeniero Manuel Becerra, a lively square, which is bordered by a lighthouse on one side and by the harbour gate on the other.

On the south shore of the peninsula, near the harbour, you'll find the Castillo de la Luz, the oldest fortress on the island of Gran Canaria.

The peninsula of La Isleta is separated from the modern part of Las Palmas by a narrow inlet. It is bordered in the south by the harbour Puerto de la Luz, one of Europe's most important harbours.

Built originally to provide jobs for the locals, this harbour has become the main container transhipment harbour of the North African region. It has also played a vital role in the prosperity of the island of Gran Canaria. Today, about 1,000 ships a month use this harbour.

Adjoining the harbour in the south is a yacht marina from where annual international Atlantic-crossing regattas set out.

Our tip:

If you explore La Isleta to the north you will reach Las Coloradas, at 239 metres the city's highest peak, from which you can enjoy a fantastic view of the sea, the mountains and the city.

Castillo de la Luz

Located on the southern coast of La Isleta, the Castillo de la Luz (Castle of Light) defended the natural harbour of Las Palmas de Gran Canaria for several centuries. Built in 1494 on top of the foundations of an existing fort from the time of the conquest by the Castilians, this solid square-shaped fortress, which was equipped with a platform for 11 cannons, nevertheless suffered severe damages during the invasion of Dutch pirates in 1599 when it was more or less burned to the ground.

Since then the two-storey building has been rebuilt, extended and improved. Indeed, in 1941 the Castillo de la Luz was declared a national historic monument. This well-preserved fortress was further restored in 1998 and serves today as a cultural and exhibition centre for national and international events.

Santa María de Guía

Santa María de Guía was formerly part of Gáldar but has since developed into a charming little town on its own. It was here where the famous and most productive of Canarian architects and sculptors, José Luján Pérez (1756 1815) grew up.

This pretty old town with cobbled streets and traditional houses is dominated by the triple-nave parochial church Iglesia de Santa María de Guía which was built in 1607. It has a neoclassical façade and houses in its interior many important works from the popular sculptor. It gives the impression of being more of a museum dedicated to the sculptor rather than of a church.

Guía is however best known for its *Queso de Flor* (Flower Cheese), made of milk mixed with the juice of the thistle-like flowers of the artichoke, giving this cheese its unusual, distinctive flavour. It tastes surprisingly good and has already won many prizes. And every year, from the last week of April to the first days of May, Guía holds the very popular *Fiestas del Queso* (Cheese Festivals).

About 5 km (approx. 3 miles) east of Guía, you'll find the pre-Hispanic Cenobio de Valerón, a group of about 300 caves, hollowed out of the soft rock on different levels. These caves were used for grain storage and religious rituals and were easy to defend because of their unique position

Gáldar

Gáldar the name derives from Agaldar, which translates as 'Royal City'. Once the centre of the Guanche civilisation, it is therefore rich in archaeological sites. The Spanish founded the post-conquest Gáldar in 1484. Previously the seat of Tenesor Semidán (latterly known as Fernando Guanarteme), one of the island's two Guanche chiefs, Gáldar takes much pride in its heritage, witnessed in the Guanche names of many of its streets. This northern town was also the capital of the island before Las Palmas de Gran Canaria.

Today, Gáldar is a largish and busy town extending at the foot of the Pico de Gáldar volcano. It has an idyllic square, the Plaza de Santiago, featuring the neoclassical *Iglesia de Santiago de los Caballeros* and is situated in front of the former site of an ancient royal court and a small Spanish fort. The construction of this vast church with three naves began in 1778 but was not completed before the middle of the 19th century. Noteworthy features are a green font from the 16th century and the statues of Christ and the Virgin Mary, both works by José Luján Pérez.

In the same square stands the *ayuntamiento* (town hall), in whose courtyard you can see an enormous dragon tree, believed to be planted no later than 1718 and therefore thought to be one of the oldest on the archipelago.

The biggest attraction of Gáldar, however, is *El Museo y Parque Arqueológico Cueva Pintada* (Painted Cave Museum and Archaelogical Park). Featuring many colourful geometric Guanche paintings, it was only discovered in 1873. After conservation works were carried out between 1970 and 1974, it was closed to the public in 1982 in order to prevent the paintings from being destroyed by the increasing humidity. It was subsequently re-opened in July 2006.

Beach lovers are advised to make a slight detour to Sardina del Norte. The miniature jewel in the crown of the beaches on the north coast, it offers a front of tantalising golden sand and delicious freshly-prepared sardines at its ample selection of restaurants.

On the road to Artenara, you'll find the Caldera de Los Pinos de Gáldar, a huge volcanic crater formed during the last volcanic eruptions on the island. From here you have wonderful views over the entire north coast.

Just 2 km (1.25 miles) north of Gáldar is another important Guanche legacy, an 11th century cemetery the Túmulo de la Guancha. In 1936 an archaeological excavation discovered the last known resting place of Guanche nobles. The bodies of 42 Guanches, believed to be the royalty of their day, are laid to rest in this tomb which is referred to as 'the royal tomb' and is built from enormous blocks of lava. There are also 30 other archeological structures at the Túmulo de la Guancha.

Agaete

Further along the north coast at the end of a steep ravine the Barranco de Agaete, where bananas, mangos, papayas, oranges, lemons and other subtropical plants and trees grow on steep slopes lies the small, but not quite sleepy, town of Agaete with its narrow streets and whitewashed houses surrounded by lush vegetation.

Many artists and art-lovers made this place their home, which also explains why you can find many art galleries here. This tranquil little town has in spite of its old age it celebrated its 500th birthday in 1981 few historic sites of interest. The oldest of which is the *Iglesia de la Concepción*, dating from 1874, opposite the Plaza de la Constitución, where you will see some attractive noble houses with carved wooden balconies. Nearby is a small botanical garden, the *Huerto de las Flores*, with many species of Canary and sub-tropical flora.

On the 4th of August one of the biggest parties on Gran Canaria, the Fiesta de la Rama, the origins of which lie in an obscure Guanche rain dance, takes place.

Puerto de las Nieves

Puerto de Las Nieves is a picturesque fishing village on the north coast of Gran Canaria. Filled with charm, Canarian character and atmosphere, it has become a popular place to visit in recent years and has been renovated into an attractive resort, ideal for a day trip or if you want to go island hopping as the ferry to Tenerife departs from its harbour.

The Paseo de los Poetas is particularly pleasant; a lovely promenade lined with seafood restaurants, craft shops and galleries. It starts at the cute, quaint, little harbour and is a great place to enjoy a stroll in the sunshine. At sunset the views are simply breathtaking, with Tenerife's Mount Teide in the distance as well as stunning countryside and pristine sea waters.

A local delicacy is served here and is too good to miss: the caldo de pescado, a stocky fish soup. Visitors are drawn to this picturesque village for its serenity and surroundings rather than the hustle and bustle of a popular mainstream resort.

The village's rich history can be seen in the tiny chapel by the main square, known as Ermita de las Nieves, which features a real treasure a 16th Century triptych (a piece of artwork in three different segments) depicting the Virgin and Child, painted by the famous

Flemish artist Joos van Cleve. During the Fiesta de la Rama, a copy of this triptych is carried in a procession to the parish church of Agaete and exhibited there.

At the southern end of this village you will find the Dedo de Dios (God's Finger). This is a 30 metre (100 ft) slender pinnacle of basalt rock rising out of the ocean, directly in front of the impressive cliffs, which are crowned by the Pinar de Tamadaba (an extensive pine forest). When Tropical Storm Delta hit in 2005, the Dedo was damaged but it still makes for an extraordinary sight and is a great photo opportunity.

Arucas

Arucas is the main town in the north of Gran Canaria, separated from the capital by the ravine Barranco de Tenoya. Dominated by the huge neo-Gothic Parish Church of San Juan Bautista, Arucas boasts some interesting historic buildings, mostly representing the architectural style of the 19th century.

Erroneously also called the Cathedral of Arucas, this majestic lava-stone church boasts a 60 metre-high tower, which is the highest church tower on the archipelago. Designed by Catalan architect Manuel Vega i March, the construction began in 1909 and stretching over several stages was finally completed in 1977. The more conventionally neo-Gothic interior features splendid stained-glass windows and retables as well as a sculpture of *Cristo Yaciente* (Christ Recumbent), the work of a local artist Manuel Ramos González (1899-1971).

Located in the *Plaza de la Constitución* (Constitution Square), you'll find two more buildings of great architectural value, one of which is the old Town Hall, which was built in 1875 and completely restored in 1932, and the other one the Municipal Market, which is also noteworthy because of its size. This has since been transformed into an upmarket shopping centre. On the opposite side of this square there is the attractive Municipal Garden, called Jardín de Hespérides, a welcoming shady place with many species of tropical trees and plants, where you can relax from your visit to the town. In *Calle de la Heredad*, a street which flanks the park and gardens, you can see one of the town's most beautiful buildings, the *Heredad de Aguas de Arucas y Firgas*, built in 1908 and home to the Water Board today.

Arucas AKA the City of Rum houses Destilerías Arehucas, the biggest rum distillery in the whole of the Canary Islands. Founded in 1884, this factory (*fábrica*) with a yearly production of more than 3.5 million litres of rum, also boasts an interesting museum where you can learn everything about the history of the factory and the rum-production process and where you will also see barrels signed by celebrities like the famous tenors Alfredo Kraus and Plácido Domingo, along with members of the Spanish royal family.

Nearby, just 1.5 km (about 1 mile) north of Arucas, you will find the Montaña de Arucas, at 412 metres the highest peak of this town. From the Michelin-listed restaurant at the top, which provides regional food and drinks, you'll enjoy great panoramic views over the island.

The people of Arucas, in common with the rest of the island, love nothing more than a good party. And none more so than on the 24th June when a fiesta celebrates the day of their patron saint, *San Juan Bautista*.

Firgas

Firgas, a small town famous for its production of sparkling mineral water, which is drawn from a spring in Barranco de las Madres, around 4 km (about 2.5 miles) away. Filling over 200,000 bottles a day, this tasty water is very popular throughout the islands.

This pleasant little town, which celebrated its 500th anniversary in 1988, features the Paseos de Canaria and de Gran Canaria, where a man-made waterfall cascades 30 metres (about 100 ft) down shallow steps in the centre of pedestrian passages laid out in 1995. On the backrests of benches at the walls of bordering houses you can see beautifully painted landscapes and historic symbols of the seven Canary Islands.

Follow this diverting promenade to reach *Firgas' Casa de la Cultura* and a neighbouring square housing both the Town Hall and the *Iglesia San Roque* where young and old meet at any time of the day.

Moya

A narrow road meandering through volcanic valleys leads to the sleepy, little town of Moya, worthwhile visiting for its impressive Neo-Romanesque church, completed in 1957, and also because it's the birthplace of one of Spain's most illustrious modernist poets, Tomás Morales.

Located at the edge of the ravine Barranco de Moya, this imposing parish church boasts two towers and in the interior some interesting pieces of sculptures including a 15th century cedar-wood figure of the *Virgen de la Candelaria* to whom this church is dedicated.

Opposite the church square stands the house where Gran Canaria's most popular poet, Tomás Morales (1884 - 1921), was born and grew up. In 1976 it was transformed into a cosy house-museum dedicated to the life and work of this poet a qualified doctor of medicine exhibiting photographs, manuscripts, first editions, paintings, his Remington typewriter and much more. Today, this museum also organises contemporary art exhibitions.

Moya is also known for one of the most popular cakes of the island, the *bizcochos lustrados* (sugared sponge cake). Do not leave without having tried them or buying some!

Valleseco

The curious thing about the name of this town, 'Valleseco' literally meaning 'Dry Valley' is that this area receives more rainfall per year than any other region on the island.

Apart from the *Iglesia de San Vicente Ferrer* whose original chapel dates from the first half of the 17th century, and the *Laguna de Valleseco* (Valleseco Lagoon), which fills with fresh water during the winter months and which was recently subjected to important environmental restoration programmes, this quiet village in the mountains would appear to offer not a lot more. Yet, it's actually a hive of agricultural activity.

During the winter months many migratory birds, including the common egret, make this area their temporary home.

Teror

In Teror, a charming little town with some of the best examples of colonial-style architecture, life has always been dominated by the 18th century *Basílica de Nuestra Señora del Pino* dedicated to Gran Canaria's patron saint. The main features of the large triple-nave interior of the Basílica are the vast Baroque altar with the richly-clothed, wooden carved figure of the Virgin, surrounded by votive gifts and symbols, many religious statues created by José Luján Pérez and five of the most significant Rococó paintings on the island.

Legend has it that in 1481 a vision of the Virgin Mary appeared to some shepherds on the top of a pine tree and since then *Nuestra Señora del Pino* (Our Lady of the Pines) played an important role in the history and the everyday life of the people of Gran Canaria. When in 1914 the Pope Pius XII proclaimed her patron saint of the island, the small town of Teror, with its sanctuary, became the religious capital of the island.

Every year, on 8th September, the *Fiesta de la Virgen del Pino* (Feast of Our Lady of the Pines) is celebrated and numerous pilgrims from all over the island come to Teror to pay reverence to the saint. This feast is not only the biggest event in the region it is also the most important religious festival on the island's calendar and the celebrations usually go on for one week.

Splendid historic houses, some of them dating from the 16th century, line the main square, Plaza de Nuestra Señora del Pino, and the Calle Real de la Plaza. Featuring lavishly-carved wooden and stone balconies, they ensure a trip to Teror is like travelling back in time.

Near the Basílica, you'll find the square Plaza Teresa de Bolívar, which was named after the wife of Simón Bolívar South America's hero in the fight for independence whose great-grandfather was born in Teror. To the right of the church is the Casa Museo de los Patrones de la Virgen, a charming building set around a courtyard and furnished in a noble 17th century style, displaying paintings, weapons, old photographs and antique furniture representing the lifestyle of the nobles of that time.

Our special recommendation for visiting Teror is on a Sunday morning as there's always a bustling local market going on, where you can both sample and buy local specialities like chorizo (a soft pork sausage) and sweets made by the nuns of the Cistercian Order.

South to West

Maspalomas has been welcoming tourists longer than anywhere else on Gran Canaria. And with its famously breathtaking dunes, that's a particularly warm welcome. Unspoilt natural beauty alongside sensitively designed modern architecture; it's a winning combination all right.

Meloneras is a luxurious resort packed with great restaurants, cafes and bars a place that is so stylish and suave. It has recently been refurbished and the finishing touches are second to none. And let's not forget the beautiful high-quality hotels that will make you feel like someone very special indeed. A touch of class.

Flasher, and altogether brasher, is its close neighbour, Playa del Inglés. Deservedly one of the most popular beaches on the island, the fun doesn't stop here when the sun goes down. That's because Playa del Inglés houses the liveliest bars and restaurants Gran Canaria has to offer.

Further west you'll find Pasito Blanco. Celebrated for its marina built at the end of the last millennium, yachting enthusiasts will cherish this maritime heaven. Pasito Blanco proves equally popular with anglers as you're able to charter big-game fishing boats here.

Heading towards Puerto Rico, is the fishing village and resort of Arguineguín. Enjoy fresh fish dishes at seaside restaurants, keep the kids entertained at the natural swimming pool or take a leisurely stroll to nearby Patalavaca. Arguineguín has long been popular with locals, and it's not difficult to see why.

Puerto Rico has established itself as the most family-friendly resort on the whole of Gran Canaria. It offers a true surf and turf experience and in the unlikely event you tire of the beach there are plenty of golf courses nearby. And if you want to pick up a souvenir or holiday gift, there's an excellent local shopping centre.

Puerto Mogán and Mogán have something in common. Both the port and the inland town offer peace and quiet. Sensitively designed, Puerto de Mogán is the perfect destination for the mature traveller or those with young children. Mogán, meanwhile, is just a great spot for getting away from it all whether it is in the acclaimed local restaurants or sitting quietly in the shade of the main square.

San Nicolás de Tolentino offers a great setting but little wow factor in terms of its buildings. More impressive are its beaches. One of which can be found in the nearby Puerto de la Aldea whose fish restaurants draw pilgrimages from Las Palmas and beyond.

Meloneras

If you're looking for a chic, sophisticated and up-market resort in Gran Canaria then Meloneras is the place for you!

Perfectly located close to the popular areas of Maspalomas and Playa del Inglés, Meloneras is on the south coast in the direction of Puerto Rico. Running north-west from the lighthouse, this resort has recently been given a major facelift and wow it's impressive!

Everything about this place has an air of luxury about it. It's attractive, trendy, affluent and above all stylish, without being over the top.

Crammed with designer shops, jewellers and high-end boutiques it's a haven for retail therapy, not to mention fine-dining. There are shopping centres, restaurants, cafés and bars running along the promenade offering cuisine from all over the world. The choice of international dishes and where to sit and enjoy a beautiful sunset are endless.

The beach itself is sandy and perfect for a spot of sun-bathing and taking a dip in the clear waters of the Atlantic - people from all over the island come to the beach here for the tranquillity if offers; you know it's good if the locals like it.

By night Meloneras really lights up. There are some great places to chill out with a glass of wine and watch the sun go down, or kick back and listen to live music playing in the background. In contrast to Playa del Inglés, Meloneras offers a more discerning kind of nightlife. You will not find lager louts here!

One of the most popular places to visit during the evening is the casino where you can try your luck on the roulette wheel or blackjack then watch the famous Legends Cabaret Show.

The hotels here ooze grandeur. They truly are wonderful boasting 4 or 5 stars, very palatial and impressive looking buildings a stay in one of these is very special indeed. Many offer top-notch cuisine from some of the best chefs on the island.

Spain-Grancanaria works with the finest hotels in the best locations all over the island and in trendy Meloneras there are three superb places to choose from. The 5-star Lopesan Villa del Conde Resort & Corallium Thalasso Hotel has excellent facilities including a world class spa offering exquisite pampering treatments, luxurious rooms with beautiful ocean views and five swimming pools within the scenic grounds. Also with 5-stars is the impressive Lopesan Baobab Resort which has a strong African theme running throughout. The accommodation is sumptuous; there are excellent facilities in the hotel, particularly for children and several on-site gourmet dining options. Located very close to the beach, this exotic hotel is a popular venue for events, particularly for guests celebrating something special.

Lopesan Costa Meloneras Resort, Corallium Spa & Casino offers guests the chance to unwind in decadent surroundings; there is definitely a sophisticated feel about this 4-star seafront hotel. An outstanding array of facilities are available including a spa centre, a selection of fine-dining restaurants, on-site casino and plenty of activities to keep younger guests entertained. Enjoy the beautiful sub-tropical gardens and uninterrupted ocean views in this stunning hotel located in one of Gran Canaria's most exclusive resorts.

And let's not forget the golfers... Meloneras has a newly built 18-hole course with lush greens, spectacular views and of course a rather nice clubhouse. Meloneras is memorable. One holiday here and you'll want to come back again and again

Maspalomas

Maspalomas, also known as the Maspalomas Costa Canaria, consists of the beach resorts of Águila, Las Burras, San Agustín and Playa del Inglés. Here you'll find a 2,000 hectare strip of land with 17 km of wonderful coastline with sand dunes, wide sandy beaches, shallow waters and an excellent all-year-round climate a paradise for beach lovers and family holidays. Maspalomas Dunes webcam.

The more up-market Maspalomas resort, with smart hotels, luxury residences and the largest golf course on the island, is separated from Playa del Inglés by a spectacular stretch of 400 hectares of dunes, which in 1994 were designated a national park. You can only cross the dunes on foot or by camel, which makes you believe you're in a different part of the world altogether. The dunes also provide a habitat for a number of rare plant species, some of which can only be found in the Canaries somehow they manage to survive in this arid environment alongside lizards and rabbits.

The sand dunes of Maspalomas are a favourite zone for nudists and the gay community so do bear this in mind when strolling along.

At the western end of this nature reserve you'll find El Oasis, which is bordered by La Charca, the remains of a sea-water lagoon bordered with palm trees, hosting many species of migratory birds from Europe stopping here on their route to Africa.

A noteworthy sightseeing attraction close to El Oasis is Faro de Maspalomas, a lighthouse built in 1886. At 65 metres tall, it dominates the area and serves as a crucial beacon for ships sailing in the region.

Since the 1960s the economy of the municipality of San Bartolomé de Tirajana has been boosted by the thriving tourism in this area. With the modern Palacio de Congresos de Maspalomas, a conference centre with a 5000+ capacity, Maspalomas has started to attract business travellers too.

But that's not all. There's so much more entertainment and fun to be found in the nearby surroundings or just a few kilometres north of Maspalomas with attractions such as Aqualand Maspalomas, (the biggest water park on the island), Holiday World (an extensive amusement park with a Ferris wheel), Palmitos Park (an ornithological park with aquarium, butterfly house and orchids), Sioux City (a Wild West theme park) and the fascinating Mundo Aborigen ("a place of cultural, social and historical interest", according to the Canarian government).

Maspalomas sounds lovely doesn't it? Here at Spain-Grancanaria we present a selection of only the crème de la crème of hotels for your delight and pleasure. Not only will you have outstanding recommendations, you will be impressed with the unbeatable value of the deals on offer throughout the Canary Islands.

In this resort we can vouch for two fantastic hotels, each displaying their own unique style and charm. The 5-star Lopesan Baobab Resort oozes class with its African theme, sumptuous rooms and fantastic facilities it really does have the 'wow factor'. The IFA Faro Hotel has a fantastic position poised on the Maspalomas beachfront; you can even listen to the waves gently lapping the shore from the comfort of your guestroom. With a 4-star rating, excellent hospitality and great cuisine, staying here is a real treat.

Playa del Inglés

Playa del Inglés (the English beach) offers sand by day and pubs and clubs galore by night. The biggest holiday complex in all of Spain, together with Maspalomas and San Agustín, Playa del Inglés is a fun-and-sun resort of high-rise hotels, shopping malls and fast-food restaurants. Created in the 1960s on, what was up to that point, barren land - it is now a tourist hyper-centre and famous throughout Europe.

In between Indian bazaars, with all sorts of goods from rags to radios, an endless amount of restaurants compete for your attention with international dishes, traditional breakfasts from half a dozen countries and anything else they can think of. Playa del Inglés is also the place where you find several huge commercial centres, the biggest of which are the Yumbo Centrum (in Avenida de España next to the Tourism

Office) and Kasbah (in Plaza del Teide) with all kinds of boutiques and shops.

Located in the heart of Playa del Inglés, the 4-star Hotel Neptuno is a perfect place to stay for guests wanting to be close to the vibrant and exciting centre. Reserve a room here and not only will you be a stone's throw from all the action, but you will enjoy sumptuous accommodation, an inviting swimming pool with no kids (this is an adults only hotel) and a wellness centre where you can pamper yourself.

For those of you who like a little more peace and quiet, Spain-Grancanaria recommends the 4-star Vital Suites Hotel & Spa, which is located a little further away from the hustle and bustle. Unwind in the spa facilities, chill out by the pool and enjoy the top class guest rooms. And golf fans will love being so close to the Maspalomas Golf Club which neighbours this hotel and offers discounts on green fees for hotel guests.

If you are looking for monuments or other cultural sights, this is not the place to be. Daylight hours can be spent on the beach or shopping but come nightfall the scenery changes completely when the bubbling family atmosphere disappears as discos and nightclubs swing into action until dawn. There are a wide range of venues, including plenty of English, German, Dutch and Scandinavian restaurants and bars.

Yet, for more spiritual needs, there is the Templo Ecuménico de San Salvador, a church providing ecumenical services in three different languages.

Should you get tired of the beach, there is an attractive pedestrian promenade, the Paseo Costa Canaria, lined with lush tropical flora and luxurious villas. It runs all along the beach linking the Playa de las Burras in the east to where the Maspalomas dunes begin.

Pasito Blanco

A short drive from the tourist resort of Playa Meloneras is the marina of Pasito Blanco.

Due to its isolated location approximately 6 km (some 3.2 miles) west of Maspalomas, this modern yacht marina, incorporating a sailing school and a private camping site, dates back to the turn of the millennium.

Pasito Blanco is a secure place to leave a boat unattended for long periods as the gate to the marina is guarded 24 hours a day. You'll also be able to find big-game fishing charters here.

The approach and entrance to the marina are straightforward and Pasito Blanco Marina (Club de Yates de Pasito Blanco) maintains a 24-hour listening watch on the marine radio service's VHF channel 12. On arrival, the skipper should report to the port office during office hours: 09.00-13.00 and 15.00-17.00 Monday to Friday and 09.00-13.00 on Saturday, tel: 928 142194.

All berths feature supplies of water and electricity which are included in the charges. There are hot water showers and toilets on the outer wharf and showers are also available in the boatyard. As usual, long-term rates are considerable lower than the daily rate and there is a 30% discount for stays over 6 months. The marina also provides a caretaker service for yachts.

Arguineguín

Arguineguín is a small town located at the end of the motorway, which was, until fairly recently, little more than a fishing village. Still a working port, Arguineguín has developed into more of a tourist resort with the usual modern hotel complexes. Yet, this little town has managed to preserve its original pleasant core with several good fish restaurants and some lively fishermen's bars at the harbour, making a visit well worthwhile.

Here, the busiest day in the week is Tuesday, when Arguineguín hosts the largest market on the island. If you want to avoid the traffic on the road, then take the regular boat services from Puerto Rico or Puerto Mogán to visit the market and have a stroll around the harbour.

There's also a pleasant coastal promenade connecting Arguineguín with the beautiful beaches and coves at Patalavaca.

Puerto de Mogán

This quaint fishing port offers a rather more subtle form of tourism than the bustling beach resorts of Playa del Inglés and Maspalomas. The waterfront, a purpose-built holiday resort, features buildings no higher than three floors and was expanded into a traffic-free village with colourful houses designed in the Mediterranean style. These houses give way to narrow alleys, all of them prettily lined with small gardens and window boxes planted with flowers, mostly bougainvilleas, in an array of colours.

Puerto de Mogán also boasts a network of pretty sea-water channels from which this port earns its 'Little Venice' nickname linking with promenades and small bridges, making a stroll around this port very relaxing.

The attractive yacht marina with its neat and tidy restaurants, stylish cafés, jazz and piano bars surrounding the local fishing fleet, which is still operating, is the perfect location for an evening walk and, what's more, a romantic sunset dinner.

Puerto de Mogán represents an ideal day out too, especially on a Friday morning when a huge and attractive market occupies the fishermen's quay. At the east of the port there lies a small, well-protected sandy beach ideal if you have children holidaying with you.

Puerto Rico

Puerto Rico is one of Gran Canaria's most popular family resorts and is situated at the mouth of a valley on the south coast of the island. Once a small fishing port, today it is a beautiful and pleasant holiday area with restaurants, an attractive promenade, plenty of sun and an amazing natural landscape.

Take a leisurely stroll along the promenade or enjoy the choice of bars, restaurants and cafés there. Stop off for a cool drink, a bite to eat and browse around the shops that are dotted around this area.

The cosy and beautiful beach sits just in front of the main walkway and is a haven for sun worshippers because of its soft golden sand and pristine calm waters. Renowned to be one of the sunniest spots on the island, Playa de Puerto Rico is the place to perfect your tan! The choice of water sports on offer here is amazing. Maybe you like the thrill of jet-skiing? Perhaps you have always wanted to try windsurfing?

Very close to this lovely beach is the Marina Suites Hotel, situated in a prime position with stunning vistas overlooking the sea. Enjoy 4-star luxury accommodation in a place that comes with a first-class recommendation from Spain-Grancanaria.

Views of the picturesque marina can be enjoyed from this fantastic hotel with its nautically-inspired design. Elegant boats are moored on the turquoise water and there is a well-known sailing centre and club based here. Over the years members have won an impressive five Olympic gold medals and deep-sea fishing thrives, evidenced in the 50+ world records obtained by fishermen setting out from here. Leisure excursions such as pleasure boat trips along the coast, dolphin watching cruises or a trip in a glass-bottomed boat to discover the underwater world, are also popular enticements for visitors.

A short walk from the marina is the water theme park Atlantida with its fun slides and thrilling rides. A major attraction, this is especially popular with families and is located next to the Puerto Rico Shopping Centre, which is home to bars, shops, fast food outlets and a disco.

In addition, if golf is your thing, you will be pleased to know there are many courses in the south of the island. The nearest is a five minute drive away in Mogán.

All in all, Puerto Rico is a popular choice among holidaymakers who love the sunshine, golden beach, plush accommodation, stunning scenery and wealth of attractions.

Mogán

Just before you reach the sleepy, little town of Mogán you will come across a windmill standing at the side of the road in the tiny hamlet of El Molino de Viento (meaning windmill). And as you enter Mogán who will see the peculiar sight of life-size sculptures representing household utensils like cups and saucers. These bizarre objects are displayed in the neat gardens and can clearly be seen from the road.

Surrounded by rugged mountains, Mogán boasts a charming central square with colourful well-kept gardens around it and a pretty church dedicated to San Antonio.

In high season, you might find a bit more activity going on in the streets, as Mogán also boasts a couple of good restaurants, including Acaymo one of the best on the island and locals as well as visitors drive up to enjoy the good food in these relaxing surroundings and to take a breath of fresh air in this tranquil mountain village.

Judging from the great amount of archaeological finds made in this area, Mogán was very populated in prehistoric times but became deserted, as it was too isolated. Specific sites of particular interest nearby include Tauro Alto, Barranco de Arguineguín, Barranquillo de la Jara, Lomo Galeón and Cañada de La Palma.

San Nicolás de Tolentino

The twisting road that leads you through a fertile valley, criss-crossed with ravines, to the small town of San Nicolás de Tolentino makes for an interesting drive! The first ravine you will pass is the Barranco de Veneguera, a valley, which in 2003 - after years of protests by environmentalists who finally prevented the valley being developed into a tourism zone was integrated into the neighbouring Parque Rural del Roque Nublo nature reserve.

The next gorge is Barranco de Tasarte, where the road becomes a little less hairy, and which ends in a little, unspoilt beach like all the Barrancos here. From the third and last ravine, the Barranco de Tasartico, on our way towards San Nicolás de Tolentino, a long and strenuous hike leads us through the Reserva Natural Especial de Güi-

Güi, an area covering 3,000 hectares of land put under protection to preserve the vegetation clinging onto the surrounding rocks.

A little bit further you will come across the natural phenomenon of La Fuente de los Azulejos named after the blue tiles that often adorn Portuguese houses. This is where oxidation has turned the rocks bluish-green, an amazing and unusual sight to see.

We finally arrive at San Nicolás de Tolentino, officially known as La Aldea de San Nicolás de Tolentino. Representing the agricultural centre of the region, here apart from plantations of orange, papaya, banana, mango and avocado - tomato growing used to be the main income. Even if the tomato production has declined due to a strong competition led by Moroccan growers, annual exports still reach about 100,000 metric tons.

Surrounded by slopes overgrown with cacti and bamboo, this miniature town features little architecture of note, with the exception of the Iglesia de San Nicolás Church. Built in 1972 on the site of an old chapel from the 18th century, it houses some interesting sculptural works created by José Luján Pérez.

Tourists flock to the nearby Cactualdea, a cacti park with thousands of cacti imported from countries like Mexico, Madagascar, Guatemala and Bolivia, set between palms, dragon trees and aloe. There's also a

Guanche Cave and a traditional restaurant serving typical Canarian dishes. Another place of interest is a large amphitheatre used for lucha canaria (Canarian wrestling) bouts.

Puerto de la Aldea

The tiny fishing port of Puerto de la Aldea, where small restaurants serve simple, but ever so delicious, fish dishes is a beautiful place to visit. South of the port, there is a long pebbled beach - Playa de la Aldea - and a pretty tiled promenade.

At the far end of the beach is El Charco (The Lagoon), which only really gets busy on weekends as well as the 11th of September when the Fiesta del Charco takes place. The origins of this festival, where locals try to catch fish with their bare hands and splash each other with water, hark back to an aboriginal past. A unique breed of fish is allowed to grow all year until just before the festival when literally hundreds of people descend on the Charco, launch themselves into the water and try to catch as many fish as they can. There are also Canarian wrestling matches and stick-fighting competitions.

Some 9 km (approx. 6 miles) further up the coast you will come across two viewpoints, the Mirador del Balcón and the Andén Verde, where you can relax a bit from what, at times, can be an extremely demanding coastal road. Perched on the edge of jagged cliffs at up to 500 m above sea level, these viewpoints allow stunning views over the north-western part of Gran Canaria.

East to South

Gran Canaria - East to South

Telde is the same distance from Las Palmas and the airport. The second city of Gran Canaria with a population of around 100,000, Telde is also the oldest recognised by papal decree way back in 1351. If you visit only one place in Telde, make it the Basílica de San Juan Bautista, a stunning Gothic church handily located on the main square.

Further south and well worth the slight detour is Valsequillo. Noted for its gastronomic delights including cheese, strawberries and wine, you can buy these products directly at the regular markets or sample them in a good selection of bars and restaurants if you can reclaim your jaw from the floor after you take in the amazing views of the surrounding countryside, that is.

Further south is Ingenio, one of Gran Canarias's more ancient towns. Perfect for a ramble, Ingenio seems a sleepy sort of place until you discover it's actually a hive of activity with the island's embroidery industry based here.

After crossing the Barranco de Guayadeque, possibly the most fertile valley Gran Canaria has to offer, you'll reach Agüimes. Small yet perfectly formed, this town showcases the typically Canarian neoclassical architecture with the Parroquia de San Sebastián, the local church and the town's finest example of this unique form of architecture.

Santa Lucía de Tirajana is a charming village with whitewashed buildings and demands your legs be stretched. As does the equally lovely San Bartolomé de Tirajana, admired even more after a shot or two of their famous liqueurs or spirits. And Fataga is the perfect place to wander around, as many consider it to be the most picturesque village in the whole of Gran Canaria

Telde

Telde is the second largest town on the island, located 13 km (approx. 10 miles) south of Las Palmas.

It is an attractive old town and was one of the two pre-Hispanic kingdoms with Gáldar. The historical core centers on the attractive Plaza de San Juan, shaded by big, old trees and surrounded by pretty colonial-style houses, painted in green and white, with elaborately-carved balconies.

Dominating this square, you'll find the large Basílica de San Juan Bautista, highlights of which are a splendid Flemish altarpiece showing six scenes out of the life of the Virgin and a statue of Christ made from corncobs by Mexican Indians a figure, which despite its height of 1.85 m only weighs 7.5 kg because of the unusual material it is made of.

Calle Inés Chemida links the Plaza de San Juan with another historic part of the town, the picturesque district of San Francisco, grouping around the Iglesia de San Francisco. Here, oval basalt pebble stones pave the narrow streets and you can still see the old, dark glazed street signs.

Calle San Fernando, named after Fernando and Juan Léon y Castillo the famous brothers, who transformed Las Palmas' harbour and who were born in Telde houses the Casa-Museo Léon y Castillo dedicated to their lives and activities as engineers and diplomats.

La Montaña de las Cuatro Puertas with relics of pre-Hispanic times is south of town halfway between Telde and Ingenio and is well worth dropping by. Situated on a hill, which the Guanches considered holy, the Cuatro Puertas consist of a main chamber with four huge entrances, which housed Telde nobility, and also might have provided a workplace for their embalmers.

Telde also boasts the widest coastal strip on the east side of the island with a broad spectrum of beaches some sandy, some pebbled lined up one after another. In this area you'll find Agua Dulce, Del Hombre, Melenara and Salinetas... to name just a few.

Valsequillo

It's well worth taking the trip towards the centre of the island to visit the picturesque village of Valsequillo. The historic centre and surrounding neighbourhoods tell a lot of this region's history, which you can learn from the Iglesia de San Miguel Arcángel, the former Cuartel de Caballería de Colmenar(Cavalry Headquarters), the district of Tenteniguada at the foot of the Roque del Saucillo and the caves of pre-Hispanic origins.

From the Mirador del Helechal, you'll enjoy an excellent vantage point with superb views over the steep cliffs and plains planted with strawberries and flowers.

This area is also known for its gastronomy, especially for its traditional cheese specialities, wines, strawberries, almonds and other agricultural products, all of which are best bought at the famous Sunday markets.

Popular fiestas in this region include the Almendro en Flor (in January and February when the almond trees are in bloom) and the Fiesta del Caballo (Horse Festival) on the 1st May.

Fresh agricultural products and exquisite cuisine in charming rural surroundings... that's what Valsequillo has to offer!

Ingenio

Positioned between the ravine Barranco de Aguatona in the north and the Barranco de Guayadeque in the south, you'll find one of the oldest towns of the island...Ingenio.

Today, a predominantly agricultural area with tomatoes being its main crop, this small town was a prosperous sugar-refining centre in the 16th century, witnessed by the remains of an old sugar cane pressing machine at the eastern end, from which the town also derives its name (Ingenio meaning sugar mill).

What this town is best known for today is its embroidery and the Museo de Piedra y Artesanía (Stone and Craft Museum) which houses pottery, wicker works and agricultural tools, as well as a collection of rocks and minerals. There is also an embroidery school, where visitors can watch how fine pieces of embroidery are created.

The attractive Plaza de la Candelaria, with modern fountains and surrounded by pretty houses with wooden balconies, provides the setting for the impressive Iglesia de Nuestra Señora de la Candelaria. This colonial-style church, which houses in its interior the image of the patron saint of the archipelago the Virgin de la Candelaria, boasts two towers and a white dome, and can be seen from far away.

You'll find one of the most important pre-historic burial grounds nearby in the Barranco de Guayadeque.

Agüimes

The town of Agüimes is separated from Ingenio by the ravine of Barranco de Guayadeque. This small, but most appealing town has a picturesque, well-preserved old centre with medieval narrow streets and pretty, ochre- or terracotta-coloured houses, dominated by the two tall towers of the Parroquia de San Sebastián located in the Plaza del Rosario. This three-nave basilica, which was declared a Historic Cultural Monument, is one of the best examples of the Canary Islands' neoclassical architecture. Featuring a vast dome with an oriental touch, it houses some statues of saints, works from José Luján Pérez.

In September, the Festival del Sur hits town. Subtitled Encuentro Internacional Tres Continentes, this is an international theatre festival with companies from South America, Africa and Europe performing. This cultural event has established itself as a highlight of the year for locals as well as visitors.

Doubtless the biggest attraction of this area, though, throughout the year remains Agüimes' Parque de Cocodrilos Zoo, a small zoological park with shows of trained crocodiles and parrots.

Along the coastline of Ingenio and Agüimes, you'll find the beaches Playa de Vargas, an ideal spot for windsurfing, and the Playa del Cabrón, one of the best diving locations on the island.

Barranco de Guayadeque

The evergreen Barranco de Guayadeque stands out as one of the most magnificent valleys of the island. Cacti, agaves, poppies, palms, Canary Island pines and almond trees, as well as more than 80 endemic species, grow in abundance on steep slopes. The neighbouring towns, Ingenio and Agüimes, get their water from a stream running through this ravine.

This valley, which in pre-historic times was the most populated on the island, provides the setting for one of the most important pre-historic burial grounds, where the dead were buried in inaccessible caves. The Guanches the original inhabitants of the Canaries - later used these caves to dwell in, to store food and as sites for fertility rituals. In the 19th century, after locals started plundering the graves and selling much of their archaeological finds to the Museo Canario in Las Palmas, this area became a designated nature reserve to protect it from further devastation.

Also home to the biggest lizard species in the world, the Lagarto Canarión, this area is a paradise for serious walkers, where there is a lot to explore in organised groups or alone. As the surfaced road continues past the Museo de Guayadeque (Centro de Interpretación Arqueológica), you can enjoy the magnificent sceneries of this valley even without much physical effort. This route passes through two cave villages where modern-day people settled to follow the footpaths of the Guanches with tiny chapels, a bar and a basic restaurant, and ends at the Tagoror, the famous cave restaurant, where both local wine and traditional folk music accompany your meal.

Santa Lucía de Tirajana

The picturesque little village of Santa Lucía will charm you with its whitewashed houses and abundance of palm trees. It's located on the upper levels of the fertile palm valley of Santa Lucía de Tirajana.

Throughout the 19th century the population of this village was very small and widely spread, so that within the confines of this municipality you also find the village of Sardina and the coastal towns of Doctoral and Vecindario. After tomato growing was introduced in the coastal areas of this municipality and also with the impact of the tourism boom in the 60s, the population grew rapidly. Many people working in the southern tourist resorts preferred to settle in this region, as property prices were less expensive.

Perched on the top of the hill stands the Iglesia de Santa Lucía, which was built in 1898 on the site of a former 17th century chapel. The imposing dome of the church looks more like a mosque when you look at it from afar.

The village of Santa Lucía also boasts a small, but notable, museum, the Museo del Castillo de la Fortaleza, displaying archaeological finds from the surroundings such as Guanche artefacts, agricultural tools, leather goods and skeletons.

Nearby, you'll discover the Fortaleza Grande, a rock formation mysteriously shaped like a fortress, which was where the Guanches made one of their last stands. Legend has it that in 1483, many Guanches refused to convert to Christianity and instead threw themselves off these rocks to their deaths. In commemoration of this historical event, every year on the 29th of April a ceremony takes place on the plateau behind it.

Along the coast, the first beach you come to is Pozo Izquierdo, one of the main World Windsurfing Championship venues. Pozo Izquierdo is also home to the Centro de Interpretación Marítima (Maritime Interpretation Centre).

San Bartolomé de Tirajana

As you head towards the centre of the island approaching San Bartolomé de Tirajana, you pass the huge volcanic crater of Caldera de Tirajana at the beginning of the Barranco de Tirajana, which is overgrown with lush vegetation.

The historic little town of San Bartolomé de Tirajana also serves as the administrative centre of the coastal regions of Maspalomas and Playa del Inglés, which makes it the most extended municipality in Gran Canaria. This region is known for its plantations of almonds, plums, peaches and cherries, which are used in the production of spirits and liqueurs. These fruits are an extra special ingredient in the San Bartolomé specialties Guindilla, a cherry liqueur, and Mejunje, a sweet concoction of honey, rum and lemon.

The triple-nave parish church Iglesia de San Bartolomé started being built in 1690, but it was consecrated almost three centuries later in 1922. In its interior it features Mudéjar-style wooden vaults and a main altarpiece with the image of Saint Bartholomew occupying the centre. Every Sunday morning a market is held in the surrounds of the church. Another church to be found in San Bartolomé is the Iglesia de Santiago de Tunte, consecrated to St. James.

The main festivals in this region are celebrated on the 24th of August, day of San Bartolomé, and the 25th of July, day of Santiago (St. James) -a major party here and all over the island.

Many of the ancient aboriginal tracks, Caminos Reales (royal roads), can to be found in this area. These old tracks were once the only means to get around in the centre of the island. In recent years many of them have been restored and re-opened to walkers and hikers in a bid to promote eco-friendly tourism. Find more information about the Caminos Reales on our Leisure & Sports pages.

If you would like to stay in a paradise retreat surrounded by lush greenery and beautiful landscapes, Spain-Grancanaria suggests reserving a room with an awe-inspiring view at Hotel Rural Paradise Las Tirajanas. This 4-star hotel is a sanctuary for the senses; be at one with nature while enjoying fantastic hospitality and sumptuous accommodation in one of the island's most beautiful places

Fataga

The small pueblo (village) of Fataga nestles in the so-called Valley of the Thousand Palms, in a picturesque setting of tall cliffs, palms and fruit trees 30 minutes north of the beach resort, Playa del Inglés.

Perched on a rock threatening to precipitate into the gorge, this enchanted mountain village with charming rural houses, palm groves and a quaint church is considered the most beautiful village on the island. Once there, you might as well visit the pretty craft shops with all sorts of handmade products to take home as souvenirs, such as shawls, pottery or wickerwork.

There are also several pleasant restaurants and bars inviting you to sit and enjoy the pleasures of life in beautiful and tranquil surroundings.

Near the village you will find the two presas (reservoirs) de Chira and Las Niñas, both set in superb surroundings, which definitely deserve a visit because of the magnificent views and tranquility these places have to offer.

On your way out of Fataga and further down south don't miss the unique experience of a camel ride in the Barranco de Fataga that's, if you dare!

Central

There is much to see in the central parts of Gran Canaria. Spain-Grancanaria has selected some of the most attractive little towns, villages and places of interest to point you in the right direction.

The Botanical Garden (Jardín Botánico Viera y Clavijo) just on the outskirts of Las Palmas, is well worth a visit. Here you will be able to stroll through a collection of beautiful plants, endemic to the Canaries and marvel at the variety of cacti and colourful flowers. Tafira, an upmarket neighbourhood just outside of Las Palmas, is home to many wealthy residents who live in large, expensive houses. There is definitely a sense of the 'rich and famous' living in this area which also has a good selection of bars and restaurants.

A few kilometres away from the Botanical Garden you can visit the Caldera de Bandama, a dormant volcano 569 metres (1,867 ft) high. Drive up to the edge of its crater, where you can enjoy stunning views.

Santa Brígida is a lovely, peaceful village with a lot of charming Canarian architecture. During your visit, check out The House of Wine

(Casa del Vino) where you can taste all the different wines the island has to offer.

Vega de San Mateo, commonly abridged to San Mateo, is close by and from this location, you have great views of the mountains and can make your way further to Pico de las Nieves, which is the highest point of Gran Canaria. Near the summit there are excellent vantage points for awe-inspiring vistas and photography.

Located in this central mountainous area is Tejeda, a popular destination, particularly on weekends. People come here to enjoy hiking and the picture-perfect panorama.

Also in the centre is Artenara, the highest village in Gran Canaria. The views are worth many pictures as well as the village itself with many of the buildings actually built into the cliff face. This attractive little rural community oozes Canarian character and should be explored if you find yourself in this part of the island.

From nature trails, romantic gardens and spectacular landscapes to lovely villages with gastronomical surprises to be discovered, the centre of the island will surely be one of the highlights during your holiday!

Tafira

Tafira Baja and Tafira Alta

In the centre of the island are Tafira Baja and Tafira Alta two wealthy suburbs of Las Palmas de Gran Canaria with magnificent residences, built in a variety of architectural styles and surrounded by beautiful gardens. With their colourful, multi-styled villas, these two up-market suburbs have managed to maintain their original colonial-style ambiance.

Tafira Alta is the favoured residential area of Las Palmas' financial elite and wealthy foreigners, combining the Italian country-house style with spacious terraces, verandas and magnificent gardens prevails. Here, at the beginning of the 20th century, the British built elegant hotels including Los Frailes where historical political meetings took place.

Upon entering Tafira Baja you'll find the Universidad de Las Palmas de Gran Canaria, founded in 1989 and built in a predominately neoclassical style albeit with some Bauhaus influences.

The highlight of Tafira Baja remains, however, the Jardín Botánico Canario Viera y Clavijo where from the moment you park, you'll be able to tune into the beauty of birdsong.

Jardín Botánico

Jardín Botánico Canario Viera y Clavijo

From the restaurant outside the main entrance you'll be able to enjoy splendid views over the whole of this fascinating botanical garden (Jardín Botánico Canario Viera y Clavijo) it was established in 1952 by the Swede Eric Sventenius, who remained its director until his death in 1973. Most of the botanical garden is laid out along a steeply sloping side of the Barranco de Guiniguada, which at one point can be crossed on a wooden bridge to reach the flatter areas. Cobbled paths leading down in steps past caves and cascades make it not the most disabled-friendly of destinations.

Named after José de Viera y Clavijo, the author of the Canarian Natural History Dictionary, this botanical garden focuses on flowers and plants endemic to the seven islands of the archipelago, inclusive of the islands belonging to the so-called Macaronesia, Madeira, the Azores and Cape Verde.

Set on terraces and growing in their natural environment, the Jardín Botánico accords each species their own space. Just past the main entrance you will find a mini laurisilva (laurel forest), which originally covered the island in pre-Hispanic times but which was later destroyed completely. Entering from the Dragonal road, you'll first encounter the Plaza de las Palmeras featuring the Canary Island Date Palm found on all islands of the archipelago.

Other highlights to look out for include the Jardín de las Islas (Garden of the Islands), which is a central lawn with several rocks where different species flourish in groups according to the Canary island they originate from and the Ornamental Garden of Macaronesia, where you can view highly decorative plants.

This is a true paradise for botanists and nature lovers absolutely worth a visit.

Opening hours:
Daily from 09.00 to 18.00 hrs - Closed on New Year's Day and Good Friday.

Caldera de Bandama

Be prepared for an interesting drive to reach Caldera de Bandama. Once you pass Tafira Alta and after some 6 km (approx. 4 miles) drive on a winding road past several vineyards, where the grapes for the popular Vino del Monte grow, you'll arrive at the stunning Caldera de Bandama, a volcanic crater 1000 m (3281 ft) in diameter and 200 m (656 ft) deep with a 569 m (1,867 ft) high peak, the Pico de Bandama, which you can drive up. This peak has an observation platform from where despite its relatively low height you can enjoy breathtaking views of the entire north and east coast and the mountainous centre in the west. With a clear sky, you might even get to see the neighbouring island Fuerteventura in the north east.

This crater - named after Dutch merchant Daniel Van Dame, who in the 17th century grew vines in the crater - features a bottom with an abandoned farmhouse and the outlines of terraced fields. If you are more of the adventurous type, you can even climb down into the crater via a steep path, which is about a 30-minute hike. Today the whole area is overgrown with palms, orange and fig trees and on the slopes of the crater thrive eucalyptus and agaves among shrubs and bushes.

South of the Pico lies the oldest golf club of all Spain, the Real Club de Golf de Las Palmas de Gran Canaria, which was founded at the end of the 19th century by members of the important and influential English colony resident on the island at that time.

The reception of the club is open daily from 08:00 to 23:00 and you can play golf from 08:00. The last game can be started at 13:00.

Santa Brígida

Due to its freshwater supplies and fertile lands, Santa Brígida became one of the first municipalities to be colonized following the conquest by the Castilians.

Located at 500 m above sea level, this pretty little town full name Villa de Santa Brígida - with picturesque narrow streets lined with eucalyptus and flowery balconies is the most exclusive residential area in the proximity of Las Palmas, with many stately villas in various architectural styles. Around the turn of the century many well-off British residents had their summerhouses here to enjoy the cooler climate and the fresh air, and it is still a favourite place for a day out for locals living in the city of Las Palmas.

In the old centre stands the parish church Iglesia de Santa Brígida, a triple-nave Gothic basilica. The third and present church was rebuilt in 1904 on the original site of a chapel from 1524. Due to the growth of the population, in 1697 this chapel was replaced by a church, which was almost completely destroyed by a fire in 1897 and of which only the tower, built in 1756, remains.

Vega de San Mateo

The small town of Vega de San Mateo (commonly called just San Mateo) is an agricultural centre located in a fertile, green valley approximately 800m above sea level.

Famous for its large cattle and agricultural markets held every weekend, it has become almost a tradition for many inhabitants from

Las Palmas to do their weekly fresh fruit, vegetable and herb shopping, as well as that of cheese and other local specialities at these markets.

Worth visiting in the centre of San Mateo is its major attraction, the Museo Etnológico La Cantonera, where a 300-year-old farmhouse has been transformed into an ethnographical museum, documenting the everyday Canarian life of yesteryear. The collections include all sorts of historic agricultural artefacts, ceramics, furniture and farming equipment. As there is also a rather good restaurant on the site, it can get quite busy here at weekends.

There is also a church with a 17th century statue of San Mateo Saint Matthew the town's patron saint.

Pico del Pozo de las Nieves

As you approach the mountainous centre of Gran Canaria, you will witness a remarkable view of the spectacular central massif and its commanding high peaks, which you may have already seen from afar. Scenic, narrow roads climb past tiny, enchanting villages, narrow terraced fields, high plateaus, deep ravines and peculiarly-shaped basalt rocks. En route you will pass lush, sub-tropical vegetation including exotic fruit and eucalyptus trees gradually substituted by pines, holm oaks, bushes and shrubs at higher altitudes.

Pico del Pozo de las Nieves, is, at 1,949 metres, the highest point of the island of Gran Canaria and also its centre. Next tallest is the iconic Roque Nublo at 1,813 metres, topped with a basalt finger protruding about 80 metres high and the Roque Bentayga, at 1,412 metres high. The two latter peaks were considered holy places by the first known inhabitants of the Canary Islands, the Guanches, who left many inscriptions, ceremonial sites and granaries in this area.

Across the centre of Gran Canaria, visitors will discover archaeological parks chronicling the lives of the island's ancestors and beautiful nature reserves created to preserve the sensitive ecosystems of these unique landscapes.

It is often much cooler up here and it can get quite misty the highest peaks often obscured by clouds but when the weather's good you'll be able to enjoy breathtaking panoramic views and you might even have the chance to make out neighbouring islands such as Lanzarote, Tenerife, La Gomera and La Palma.

Our tip:

Be sure to take some warmer clothing as the cloud and altitude can make this part of the island much cooler.

Cruz de Tejeda

The village of Tejeda is the second smallest on the island. It is home to the nearby **Cruz de** Tejeda (Cross of Tejeda), a sombre carved stone cross on a mountain pass at 1580 m (5184 ft) above sea level, marking the geographical centre of Gran Canaria.

At this popular sightseeing attraction, you'll find bustling restaurants and bars, shops selling souvenirs and other local specialities, including great honey, and a man offering donkey rides to children. This is a good place to sit back, relax and enjoy a cup of coffee. If you crave peace, then you should avoid this area at weekends, as this is also a favourite place of excursion for the locals.

The high peaks will obviously attract serious walkers and climbers but this area also offers relatively short and easy walks to tempt the less energetic for a pleasant stroll amid this dazzling scenery. Whilst some of these walks are new, most of them are Caminos Reales (royal paths), ancient tracks traversed by the Guanches the first known inhabitants of the Canary Islands - to get around the centre of the island.

The village of Tejeda is surrounded by terraced cornfields, orchards and vegetable cultivations and nestles at about 1000 m (3281 ft) above sea level. It sits in the slopes of a crater and boasts many archaeological remains such as graves, caves, rock engravings and paintings.

Without the upswing of tourism in this area, this village would have been deserted long ago, as it is not possible to live only on agricultural cultivations in this barren land. As it is, this village has halved in size.

However, Tejeda provides a pleasant stopping place for lunch and while you are here try or buy some of the delicious, local almond sweet specialities Bienmesabe (literally: 'It tastes good to me') and marzipan.

When almond trees bloom during the first two weeks of February, Tejeda is at its prettiest an occasion marked by the popular Almond Tree in Flower fiesta

Artenara

A difficult but beautiful road leads you to the village of Artenara, which at an altitude of 1270 m (4167 ft) is the highest village of the island and also one of the oldest. A Christ statue with widespread arms, reminiscent of the famous Rio de Janeiro figure, welcomes visitors.

Clinging to the mountainside, this peculiar village is doubtless the most spectacular of the island with many of its houses built in the solid rock of caves dating from prehistoric times. Although some of them with their painted façades look almost like ordinary houses, and most of them are equipped with all modern amenities.

You shouldn't miss seeing the cave church La Ermita de la Cuevita, which houses the statue of the Virgen de la Cuevita, who is celebrated from the 15th August with a big fiesta. If it weren't for the bell above the entrance, you would have difficulty recognising it as a church. The more conventional church of the village is the Iglesia de San Matías.

Near Artenara, about 12 km to the west (7.5 miles) and worth a visit even when the weather is misty starts the natural reserve of Pinar de Tamadaba, the largest pine forest of the island. After travelling around the Pico de Tamadaba (1444 m/4738 ft), you'll enjoy spectacular views of the Caldera de Tejeda, the west coast and Tenerife's Teide. On misty days the pine forest changes into an enchanted fairytale scene with enormous boulders lying between the trees and the lichen, which hang down from the branches like greenish-yellow veils. This nature park is a true paradise for all walkers and nature lovers.

What to Do
What to do in Gran Canaria

When it comes to Gran Canaria, it's impossible not to think of the beach, lots of beach. This island has some of Europe's most beautiful beaches, either sandy or pebble, all different but all equal when it comes to the best conditions, fun and sun. Whether you are looking for more crowded and lively beaches or more family or secluded beaches, it's easy to find those best suited to you.

With excellent weather conditions throughout the year, in Gran Canaria you can practise several sports, especially sea sports, as bodyboarding, surfing or water skiing. If you prefer to have your feet (well) on the ground, you always have the possibility of playing golf, horseback riding and hiking or, if you would like something more extreme, climbing!

Due to lower taxes, Gran Canaria is synonymous with shopping! From clothing stores and brand accessories to commercial areas selling electronic products, in Gran Canaria there is everything, not to mention the many shopping centres that exist there, where you can find good prices, good brands and quality!

Of course you should also try local cuisine in the huge variety of existing restaurants, a great hobby for people who like to taste traditional recipes. In Gran Canaria, the traditional cuisine of Spanish origin merges with African and Latin American influences. Don't miss it!

On this island, there are several museums and very interesting cultural centres, especially in Las Palmas, as well as various events throughout the year, many of which are international, such as the Las Palmas de Gran Canaria International Film Festival.

And, at the end of a day full of discovery and adventure around the island, there is nothing like experiencing the very famous nightlife of Gran Canaria, all night long! Here, you'll find discos, pubs, nightclubs and bars for every taste, some with live music performances. However, if you prefer quieter environments or, if you like to gamble, there are two casinos on the island, one in Las Palmas and one in San Agustín.

As you can see, in Gran Canaria there are all sorts of things to do and have a good time. Just browse our guide and discover enjoy and have fun!

Beaches

Beaches of Gran Canaria
The magical island of Gran Canaria has 230 kilometres of coastline and some of the most beautiful beaches in Europe. Big ones, small ones,

sandy ones, rocky ones, they come in all shapes and sizes and provide the perfect setting for a fun-packed holiday in the sun.

Maybe you love to sit in peace and quiet listening to the sound of the waves? Perhaps you prefer a lively alternative and want a choice of activities? Whether you are travelling with children, looking for a secluded nudist beach, want a romantic retreat with your loved one or are planning a party with a group of friends there is something to suit everyone's taste.

Here at Spain-Grancanaria we provide in-depth details so you can make the right choice. From the inspiring sights of the Maspalomas sand dunes, the ever-popular Playa del Inglés, the romantically named Playa de Amadores (Lovers' Beach), or the peace and quiet of Playa Taurito or San Agustín, we have a list of the best the island has to offer.

We will point you in the right direction to enjoy water sports, including jet-skiing, wind-surfing, big-game fishing and scuba diving. Puerto Rico is a great place to take a boat trip along the coast and the capital city of Las Palmas de Gran Canaria is home to the popular Playa de las Canteras, which has a fantastic stretch of golden sand and clear blue waters. If you fancy learning how to ride the waves, surf schools are also located here. Nearby is Playa de las Alcaravaneras, a cosy beach next to a harbour packed with glamorous yachts

By clicking on the menu to the left, you will find some of the most popular beaches, not to mention a wide selection of fantastic hotels recommended by Spain-Grancanaria. Our informative, detailed and colourful beach guide gives you all the information you need to make the perfect choice for the perfect holiday. What are you waiting for? Gorgeous sunshine, crystal clear waters and luxurious hotels are just a click away.

Las Canteras

Playa de las Canteras is a huge stretch of golden sand located right in the heart of Las Palmas de Gran Canaria. More than 3 kilometres long, it is a popular choice for tourists as well as residents of the city and is protected by a natural reef called La Barra. This allows visitors to enjoy a swim in tranquil waters while surfers ride the waves in the south tip. People flock to this fantastic beach because it has ideal conditions for all kinds of water sports, provides a safe sandy environment for families and is simply a great place to relax in the sunshine.

The area south of Playa de las Canteras, where the natural rock barrier finishes, is also known as La Cicer. This spot is packed with shops selling all kinds of water sports equipment and accessories, as well as surf schools offering advice, courses and camps for all levels of experience. Along the beach is the bustling Paseo de las Canteras promenade where you will find lots of shops, open-air restaurants, snack bars and cafés. Sit and enjoy some tapas, people-watch over a cool drink and be amused by the street entertainers.

If you are looking for a metropolitan city experience, complemented by a beautiful beach, then Spain-Grancanaria highly recommends a stay in the deluxe five-star Hotel Santa Catalina, which is close to Playa de las Canteras. A free shuttle service runs from the hotel to the beach every day, so all you need to do is pack a beach bag and go. We also recommend two other exceptional hotels which are very close to Playa de las Canteras AC Hotel Gran Canaria and Hotel Cristina Las Palmas.

Playa de las Alcaravaneras

Playa de las Alcaravaneras is a beach located in the capital city of Las Palmas de Gran Canaria. Finding the perfect spot to relax on this stretch of golden sand is easy, no matter what day of the week you visit.

If you are feeling energetic, why not have a game of beach volleyball? Usually the water here is very placid so it's a great place for activities like sailing and canoeing. Kiosks sell refreshments and there is a good selection of cafés and bars nearby. Also, there are sunbeds and showers on the beach.

South of the beach is the Varadero Sailing Club and to the north is the chic Real Club Náutico (Royal Sailing Club), where you are guaranteed to spot some glamorous ocean-going yachts and maybe a millionaire or two.

Avenida Marítima is the place to go for a jog, bike ride or a long stroll as it runs the district of Vegueta to the peninsula of La Isleta.
Buses travel to Playa de las Alcaravaneras frequently from most of the major resorts and are cheap and reliable. Follow signs for car parks which are relatively inexpensive.

If this beach in a superb city location is what you are looking for, Spain-Grancanaria suggests a stay in the luxurious Hotel Santa Catalina. A complimentary shuttle service runs from the hotel to nearby Playa de las Canteras, a beautiful beach of pristine water which neighbours Playa de las Alcaravaneras.

Playa de San Agustín

Playa de San Agustín is a very relaxing beach, much quieter than Playa del Inglés and Maspalomas. Visitors looking to get away from the crowds will love this dark-coloured sandy beach a place where you have a lot of room to spread out, not to mention chill out. It does get a little busier at weekends when residents take advantage of having such a pleasant and tranquil place on their doorstep.

The beach is about 670 metres long, it has a gentle slope and is well protected against the waves. This creates ideal conditions for snorkelling and scuba diving. There are also some excellent seafood restaurants to be found on the promenade, as well as a selection of cafés, bars and shops. Shower facilities are located just off the beach. Buses run to this resort and there is a car park.

Does Playa de San Agustín sound like the kind of beach you like? Well, just a short walk away are two fantastic hotels; Meliá Tamarindos and Gloria Palace San Agustín Thalasso & Hotel. Both come highly recommended by Spain-Grancanaria.

Playa del Inglés

Bordered by the beaches of San Agustín in the east and Maspalomas in the west, the 2.7 kilometre long Playa del Inglés lays claim to being one of the most famous beaches in Europe. Thanks to Gran Canaria's mild climate and the 'feel good factor' visitors find here, it is extremely popular throughout the year and it's also the busiest tourist destination in the whole of Spain. This fun-and-sun beach offers all sorts of leisure and sports activities including jet-skiing, sailing, windsurfing, water-skiing and many more. Basically, whatever you feel like doing... you'll find it here!

There are plenty of public conveniences and showers along the beach, as well as kiosks selling cold drinks, ice-creams and other refreshments. People with disabilities will find various access points where ramps go down to the sand.

Got a great tan already? Then, take a stroll along the attractive pedestrian promenade, the Paseo Costa Canaria, which is lined with lush tropical flora and luxurious villas. It runs adjacent to the beach linking Playa de las Burras in the east to the beginning of the Maspalomas sand dunes. There is a nudist area close to the dunes and a section that is popular with the gay community near Bar 7.

For a meal or refreshing drink head to Paseo Marítimo, which is a 2 kilometre promenade packed with restaurants, snack bars, fast food outlets, amusement arcades, Irish pubs, German beer houses, internet cafés and souvenir outlets. It is a great place to shop and is covered with awnings to protect you from the heat.

Is this the type of lively and vibrant beach you are looking for? Spain-Grancanaria can recommend Hotel Neptuno, which is ideally positioned to take advantage of the beach and famous nightlife, which includes pubs, bars, cabaret clubs and a casino.

Maspalomas

Maspalomas is simply beautiful and needs to be seen to be believed! Fine white sand and wind-sculpted dunes set against the blue sea are truly an amazing sight. Of course a beach this lovely is going to be popular, especially where the sunbeds are located.

The dunes can be reached by walking through a large arched entrance on Avenida de Tirajana. Walk down a short lane and you will be in the right place. Remember to bring a towel and flip-flops as the sand can get very hot. Every 100 metres or so there are kiosks selling refreshments.

You'll find Maspalomas beach divided into four areas: the first perfect for families and kids, the second and the fourth are nudist zones and the third is popular with the gay community.

Maspalomas beach is a true paradise for all beach and fun lovers, for families with children as well as sun worshippers, especially if you want to get away from the cold north European winter!

Like Playa del Inglés, this beach also offers everything you would look for to enjoy a fabulous day on the sand and in the sunshine. There are all sorts of sports and leisure facilities available including showers as well as lots of beach bars, restaurants and shops. If you would like to go scuba diving, go out on a pedalo or hire a jet-ski, it's all here for you to enjoy. There are not many shaded areas, so it's a good idea to hire a sunshade so you can get out of the sun for a while.

Buses will drop you off close to the dunes and camel trips are available at the western end of this magnificent natural attraction. There is also plenty of free, on-street parking nearby as well as a car park.

Do you love the idea of a holiday in marvellous Maspalomas or nearby Meloneras? Spain-Grancanaria has a selection of top-class hotels that we highly recommend. Lopesan Baobab Resort, Lopesan Vila del Conde Resort, Vital Suites Hotel & Spa, Lopesan Costa Meloneras in Meloneras and IFA Faro Hotel in Maspalomas.

Playa de Puerto Rico

Puerto Rico is renowned for being the sunniest spot in Gran Canaria, so if you like it hot - this is the place to be!

During high season, the resort is bustling with holidaymakers who come to enjoy a day out on its small and beautiful beach. In addition, Puerto Rico offers a wide selection of watersports activities, ranging from jetskiing, sailing, diving, big-game fishing and windsurfing, to leisure excursions such as pleasure boat trips along the coast, dolphin-watching cruises or trips in glass-bottomed boats to discover the rich underwater life of the area.

This resort really does have a family friendly feel to it and you will find lots of children playing on the golden sand. A gentle breeze is always blowing and the sea is calm, offering ideal conditions for a dip in the warm waters of the Atlantic.

A popular public swimming pool is situated a short distance from the beach amidst the exotic plants and flowers of a lush tropical garden. Other attractions include golf courses, a water park featuring entertainment for people of all ages and a handy shopping centre nearby.

The resort provides abundant amenities, with plenty of beachfront bars and cafés, easy parking, readily available sunbeds, sunshades and numerous shower facilities. There is also wheelchair access onto the beach. Local buses run from all major destinations and are cheap and reliable.

Puerto Rico is a great resort with a fantastic beach. If you like the sound of it, Spain-Grancanaria recommends a stay in the Marina Suites Hotel, which is just a few minutes away from the inviting beach.

Playa de Amadores

Nestled between Puerto Rico and Puerto Mogán on the south-west coast of Gran Canaria lies the glorious beach of Playa de Amadores.

This extensive bay, well-protected from the ocean, boasts an 800 metre stretch of golden sand and crystal-clear waters. Peaceful and relaxing, this is a favourite choice for couples looking for a romantic setting to spend a day in the sunshine so it's no surprise that Playa de Amadores means lovers' beach.

Ball games and listening to loud music are not allowed and although the vibe is quiet, families spend time here as the sand provides perfect conditions for small children to run around and play safely. Refreshing drinks, tapas and succulent seafood are on offer from a good assortment of bars and restaurants situated directly behind the beach.

Playa de Amadores was given the prestigious Blue Flag award in 2004, an accolade for beaches which have achieved high standards in water quality, environmental education, safety and management. There are shower facilities on the beach and buses run to the resort frequently from most areas and are a cheap way to travel. Inexpensive car parking is also available nearby.

This beach sounds great, doesn't it? If you fancy staying at this resort, Spain-Grancanaria recommends the Gloria Palace Royal Hotel & Spa and/or Gloria Palace Amadores Thalasso & Hotel. Both are just 200 metres from Playa de Amadores and have stunning views of the ocean.

Our tip: Playa de Amadores is a great vantage point to watch the sun disappearing behind the volcanic Mount Teide on the neighbouring island of Tenerife a truly breathtaking sunset.

Playa de Mogán

Puerto de Mogán, the most westerly holiday resort on Gran Canaria's southern coast, is a picturesque port, a charming fishing village, a marina and chic holiday destination all rolled into one. The stretch of golden sand on this excellent and well-protected beach, makes it a favourite with families. The clear water is calm and the sea around the breakwater is a great place for snorkeling as there is a variety of fish to spot. Also, visitors can explore the fascinating underwater world by taking a trip on a yellow submarine or spending some time on a deep-sea fishing boat and catch world-record-sized tunas or marlins. There are sunbeds, sunshades, pedalos and canoes for hire and kiosks offering cool drinks and snacks.

This is an up-market holiday resort, aiming to offer quality over quantity for discerning holidaymakers who prefer relaxing surroundings to hustle and bustle.

Away from the beach is a network of canals and bridges, which is why Puerto de Mogán is often described as 'Little Venice'. Visitors can enjoy a pleasant stroll around the port, where there is a good selection of shops and superb fish restaurants.

There are places to park on the road as well as a car park close to the beach. Buses run frequently and there is a taxi rank.

A five minute drive away is the lovely picturesque beach of Playa Taurito, a soothing spot to relax in the sunshine. This area is surrounded by stunning cliffs, has calm warm waters and several restaurants close to the soft stretch of sand.

The experts at Spain-Grancanaria know a thing or two about hotels. We work alongside the best establishments in inviting locations all over the Canary Islands to guarantee your dream holiday experience. Here you will find the wonderful 4-star Hotel LTI Valle Taurito, which offers comfortable accommodation and exciting activities for the whole family. It is a short stroll from the beach and also overlooks the Lago Oasis water park, a fun-filled attraction for all ages.

Playa Taurito

Soft sand and water sparkling in the sunshine are what visitors will find at the beautiful Playa Taurito. Nestled in between Puerto Mogán and Puerto Rico on Gran Canaria's southern coast, this beach is a great spot for holidaymakers looking to relax. It's a wonderful place to get away from the hustle and bustle and enjoy the intimate surroundings of this oasis of peace and tranquillity.

Close to the beach are a selection of cafés, restaurants, shops and snack bars. A range of water sports and activities, including fishing, jet-skiing, diving and a selection of boat trips are available from nearby Puerto Rico.

Buses run to Playa Taurito from most places on the island and there is a large underground car park and a taxi rank.

Are you feeling tempted by Taurito? If so, Spain-grancanaria can recommend a stay in Paradise Valle Taurito, an attractive hotel situated close to the beach.

Playa Meloneras

Imagine yourself relaxing on the sand, listening to the waves gently splashing the shore... sounds great, doesn't it? Well, this is exactly the sort of soothing ambience you will experience at the Playa de

Meloneras, a lovely beach located in southern Gran Canaria. The warm waters are calm and great for swimming, the sand is golden and soft under your feet... perfect conditions for a day on the beach, lapping up the sunshine which can be enjoyed all-year round on the beautiful Canary Islands.

Located fairly close to the impressive sand dunes of Maspalomas, Playa de Meloneras is a popular choice for those seeking tranquillity, as it does not get overcrowded. Families visit this 500 metre (1,640 ft) stretch of sand, groups of friends hang out on sunbeds and courting couples walk hand in hand taking in the views of the ocean. There is definitely a 'feel-good factor' in the air.

A short walk from the beach is the superb Lopesan Villa del Conde Resort & Corallium Thalasso hotel, which offers 5-star accommodation, outstanding facilities and spectacular views. Staying in this plush palatial hotel is a real treat and comes with the Spain-Grancanaria seal of approval.

Just off the beach there are several restaurants, bars and cafés serving cool drinks, snacks and a choice of international food, including a particularly good Spanish restaurant that is renowned for its paella. From here you can take a leisurely stroll along the chic promenade until you reach an up-market area packed with boutiques and designer-label outlets. This is the main resort of Meloneras which has been given a complete makeover, earning it the impressive reputation as one of the most elegant and attractive locations in the south of the island.

Nestled in this stylish area is another great hotel, which we guarantee will delight and amaze. The 4-star Lopesan Costa Meloneras Resort, Corallium Spa & Casino, is set in stunning sub-tropical landscaped gardens, with its own casino, several gourmet restaurants, spa facilities and luxurious suites. We also recommend another hotel in this trendy area. Lopesan Baobab Resort is a 5-star hotel with an African theme, 8 swimming pools, exotic gardens and deluxe accommodation. Families are well catered for here with a selection of activities for children including Panchi World, an exciting leisure park with a large playground, fun stage performances and water games which will keep the kids entertained for hours.

Buses run to and from Playa de Meloneras frequently and several car parks can be found in the resort, which also has good access for disabled people

Leisure & Sports

Leisure & Sports in Gran Canaria

Gran Canaria has perfect weather conditions for all kinds of outdoor sports all year round, helping you get fit rather than fat. Whatever your favourite sport or pastime on your holidays, you'll find the opportunity to do it here.

If you are the type of person who likes to compliment your relaxation on the beach with a little light exercise, not to mention bags of fun, then Gran Canaria has a catalogue of sports and leisure activities on offer.

Let's start with water sports. As you can imagine the list is endless… from water-ski-ing to surfing, deep sea fishing to paragliding, it's all here for you water babies! Many of the beaches in the more popular resorts offer holidaymakers the chance to hire jets skis, pedal boats, surf boards, or the easier option of body boards. And resorts like Playa del Inglés, Maspalomas, Meloneras, Puerto Mogán and Puerto Rico, offer all types of excursions including taking a trip on a yellow submarine, whale and dolphin watching boat trips and much more.

For the really active among you there are other sports available on the island. Fancy a bit of rock Climbing? Maybe a spot of horse riding? It's a not a problem, we can direct you to the places where these kind of sports are available.

Walking and rambling is big on the island too. There are plenty of specific routes you can follow some of them require you to be pretty energetic and have the right kind of footwear, especially when you go up into the mountain regions. Other routes require less exertion and offer you some breathtaking views.

In total contrast, maybe your idea of leisure activities is less sport orientated and the only walking involved is strolling around the shops! Well, there are plenty of chances for a spot of retail therapy too.

Just browse through these pages and find out about everything this amazing island has to offer.

Leisure

Leisure in Gran Canaria

There is so much fun to be had on the wonderful island of Gran Canaria, that in many ways you are spoilt for choice! One thing is for sure, this small and extraordinary paradise is packed with leisure pursuits guaranteed to bring you enjoyment, amusement and pleasure. It doesn't matter how old or young you are, there is something for everyone, including many fascinating historical and cultural sites.

Visitors can hire a car by checking out our low cost car rental site Discount Rent A Car and explore the island's arid and exotic landscape. Many theme and leisure parks are nestled within this terrain and will suddenly appear out of nowhere. Head straight for them as they promise an adventurous, fun-packed day out!

More than 40 per cent of Gran Canaria's territory is protected, which means it cannot be developed. As a result, there are lots of great places for walking and hiking, especially on the Caminos Reales (royal roads or pathways). This ancient network of paths has been restored and re-opened for the public to enjoy. Not only can you stroll through them at your leisure, there's also the chance to appreciate some great views, take beautiful photographs and enjoy the flora and fauna along the way.

Favourable Atlantic winds, diverse marine life and warm water provide excellent conditions for the practice of all kinds of water sports throughout the year. Many companies, clubs and associations offer visitors the opportunity to try whale watching, sailing, windsurfing, big-game fishing and many other activities. Impressively, Gran Canaria has been home to around 30 world champions in several sailing disciplines and six Olympic Gold medallists... In addition, there have been more than 50 world record-size catches in deep sea fishing achieved off ports on the east and south coast.

Gran Canaria has become a favourite winter training centre for many European sports clubs due to its mild year-round climate. Some of the hotels even provide specialised sports facilities or offer activities including golf, tennis, sailing and windsurfing through professional clubs.

The trade winds and mountainous terrain make Gran Canaria a favourite destination for extreme sportsmen and women with hang-gliding, climbing and paragliding particularly popular. So, if you crave an adrenalin rush, you won't have to look far to locate one of the many companies that offer thrill-seeking activities.

For golf lovers, leisure time is synonymous with playing a few rounds. There is a wealth of lush greens dotted all over the island, many of which overlook the ocean.

Walking & Hiking

The good thing about Gran Canaria is that, if you tire of beaches and water sports, there's also plenty to do on land. One leisure activity that has greatly increased in popularity recently is walking or for those who like to strain themselves a bit more hiking/trekking.

In an attempt to diversify tourism on the island, the Cabildo Insular de Gran Canaria (Regional Government) invested in the recovery of the Caminos Reales (royal roads) and re-opened them to the public. These ancient paths, once the only means to get around the inner section of the island, centre on Cruz de Tejeda and radiate out from there to cover big parts of the island. Almost 66,000 hectares of the island are protected land which these old tracks provide access to. Some of these walks are on newly-built paths and there are some challenging ones with serious climbs, but there are also a series of relatively short and easy walks.

Conditions in the mountains can be very different from those on the coast, so ensure you are prepared for abruptly-changing weather conditions and commence your trek equipped with strong shoes, warm clothing, food, plenty of water, sun block and a good map. Also, we would advise you to never walk alone in these often quite deserted and rough areas in case of any mishap. It's also a good idea to carry a mobile phone with you, should you need to use it in case of any emergency.

Walking or hiking is a great way of exploring less-known, unspoiled landscapes and the dazzling beauty of the ancient Gran Canaria.

Camel Safari

No, this isn't a wind-up and yes, you're still visiting the Gran Canaria guide. Believe it or not there are camel excursions available here.

You can jump on the back of an exotic dromedary and roam around the famous Sahara-like sand dunes of Maspalomas if you're in the south of the island.

Or you can enjoy camel rides, at the Camel Safari Park located near the attractive village of Fataga. After a brief introduction about the life of a camel, you will enjoy a ride through the beautiful valley of Fataga, a camel show and finally a delicious lunch. If you're lucky you can pose for a photograph with the camels and you might even get a kiss!

The leisure company that offers this service is located within a park, where you will find a wide variety of flowers and animals as well as an impossible-to-resist swimming pool. A great day out.

Horse riding

Horse lovers can go for a leisurely trot, comfortable canter or adventurous gallop at the riding school of the Real Club de Golf in Bandama in Santa Brígida, Las Palmas. In addition to the golf club, there are stables here where holidaymakers can sign up for a lesson.

In the south of the island, you can also book riding lessons and trekking tours at Rancho Park, near Playa del Inglés (on the way to Palmitos Park). Here, you will also find a children's park and a family-friendly restaurant.

And in Maspalomas, the Canyon Horse Farm offers guided tours through trails and beautiful landscapes. Riders of all levels can enjoy this outing in the sunshine.

Sioux City, a theme park that re-creates the Wild West, has plenty of horses that are part of the exciting show. This great adventure park in Maspalomas has teamed up with the company Animal Encounters to give you double the enjoyment; sit back and watch the show then saddle up and ride out on a guided tour.

For more information about horse riding clubs and lessons, ask at the reception of your hotel. The travel experts from Spain-Grancanaria work alongside only the best 4 and 5-star hotels on the island who are always willing to offer professional advice and assistance..

Rock Climbing

An excellent all-year-round climate and an exceptional volcanic terrain with magnificent high peaks provide Gran Canaria with ideal conditions for practicing non-winter mountain sports, of which rock climbing has become one of the most popular in recent years. This has led to a growing number of enthusiastic climbers coming to the island and climbing school sites and clubs appearing everywhere.

Volcanic eruptions and erosion created a paradise for all lovers of this sport, with rugged rock formations, vertical cliffs, gullies, crests, cauldrons, rock needles, cracks, chimneys, wedges, overhangs. everything a serious climber could wish for.

There are climbing sites to be found all over the island, although the most popular ones and also climbing schools are located in areas with good access possibilities and the best rock compositions. Recommended rock needles to climb include Roque Nublo (the first climbing site to be developed on the island with 12 excellent routes and endless difficulties), El Palmés in El Toscón de Tejeda, Betancuria in Ayacata or Narices at the foot of the north face of Roque Bentayga (where there are some climbing restrictions due to the archaeological importance of this site).

Close to El Nublo stands the rock circus of Ayacata, a sanctuary of traditional climbing with the biggest number of classical routes of different lengths and difficulty degrees. Elsewhere, there's Tamadaba, an ancient mountain massif with vertical cliffs in the north west. Other enthralling climbing sites include Costa Ayala, Bañaderos and Las Meleguinas.

The leading site for sports and boulder climbing in the south, La Sorrueda, near Santa Lucia in the Tirajana gorge, attracts the most climbers. Along with Fatagonia and the southern gullies of Berriel and Ayagaures.

You can climb almost everywhere on the island, with the exception of some publicly-owned places, military terrains or sites of special ecological sensitivity. Nevertheless, all climbers need to respect, preserve and in no way disturb the natural environment and habitats wherever they climb.

Be aware that sports climbing a sport with many risks requires you to have certain documents for your own safety such as a federation licence, insurance policy covering civil liability, accidents, etc. In order to be fully prepared, we recommend getting in touch with the Canary Island Federation of Mountaineering and Climbing before your departure.

Karting

Gran Karting Club was built with both grown-ups and children very much in mind. If you love the idea of speed then look no further than this place!

It has 2 tracks, one is 650 metres and the other is 990 metres. Drivers can reach speeds of up to 80km an hour - enough to satisfy the most adventurous.

The junior track (650 metres) is ideal for those aged between 12 and 16 while 10 year olds will surely enjoy the mini-bikes. There is also a children's track with mini-karts for kids aged 5 years upwards.

Location: Carretera Gral. Del Sur Tarajalillo (10 minutes from Playa del Inglés)

Fun & Theme Parks

Gran Canaria's spectacular beaches combined with a very attractive all-year-round climate represent for millions of visitors the best reason to come to this great island every year! Beach lovers of all age groups find excellent conditions to enjoy themselves with their favourite holiday occupation in or on the water or ... simply to recharge batteries by soaking up the sun on a sandy beach.

But if you or your children get tired of the beach or if you have to stay out of the sun for a while because you've got too much of it Gran

Canaria has loads of other fun-generating pastimes to offer. Maybe you fancy a day out at a water park (Parque Acuático Oasis Lago Taurito) or would like to visit the funfair at Holidayworld. Whatever your tastes, start navigating and we're sure you'll find something that will interest you and your children for a pleasant day out full of fun and distraction.

Aqualand Maspalomas

Aqualand Maspalomas provides one of the perfect places for a family day out. At 130,000 sq. metres it's the biggest water park in Gran Canaria and provides fun for each and every member of the family with the most amazing aquatic entertainments.

Open all year round, this water park's pools alone cover an area of 5,300 sq. meters and it boasts 33 slides and 13 fun attractions including Surf Beach, Congo River, Crazy Race, Kamikaze, Rapids, Aquamania, Twister, the exotic mini-park Polynesia, mini-golf … just to name some of them. Mamut is a firm favourite where you whizz down a slide on a four-person raft and Adrenalina, is a double-rubber-ring ride. The latest attraction is not for the faint-hearted. Boomerang is a ride where you sit on a floating ring and ride down a vertical drop!

Facilities you'll find here include self-service restaurants, a pizzeria, coffee bars, shops, changing rooms, extensive gardens and free parking.

Closing time is strict, with rides closing half an hour before to ensure everybody's out on time.

Opening hours: everyday from 10.00 to 17.00. Open all year round, except in very bad weather conditions.

Location: near Maspalomas on the road to Palmitos Park.
Ctra. Palmitos Park, Km 3, 35100, Maspalomas, Gran Canaria
Note: There are height restrictions on some of the rides.

Atlántida, Puerto Rico

Famed for its numerous bathing facilities, Puerto Rico enjoys an unrivalled popularity amongst families with children. So it makes sense to have a wonderful aqua park based here a perfect day out for all of the family.

Atlantida is a new water theme park located next to the commercial centre in Puerto Rico. As the name suggests it is based on the ancient Amazon River valley, believed to have been found by explorers 4,000 years ago.

It has previously been an aqua park but has been completely transformed recently and is now a major attraction on the island. It has loads of fun slides including the kamikaze and rapid river, plenty of sun beds, parasols, café, restaurant, shops and much more.

All in all, great fun for the whole family for a day away from the beach.

Opening hours: everyday from 10.00 to 17.30 during winter and until 18.30 in the summer.
Location: Avda. Tomás Roca Bosch, 9, Puerto Rico
PLEASE NOTE: The Atlántida Water Park in Puerto Rico is closed

Palmitos Park

Gran Canaria's most popular family attraction, Palmitos Park, is a sub-tropical oasis in a verdant valley of palm trees, featuring more than 200 species of birds, including the tiny hummingbirds, toucans, peacocks, hornbills, cranes, flamingos and macaws, among other attractions such as an aquarium, a butterfly house, a cacti garden, an orchid house...the list goes on.

Palmitos Park boasts a number of must-see attractions and you should estimate at least a couple of hours or even half a day to wander around the park and take in all the sights and sounds. Particularly recommended are the breathtaking bird-of-prey shows, where eagles, owls and peregrine falcons swoop down over the audience in free flight.

Other spectacular attractions not to be missed are the parrot shows, where you'll see these intelligent birds perform an amazing variety of tricks, from riding bicycles to doing jigsaws, painting pictures and counting to ten. Popular displays like this help to fund serious conservation programmes that involve the many endangered species living in the park.

The Orchid House creates an ideal and unique habitat for hundreds of orchids in multiple shapes and colours. This is the biggest orchid collection in the Canary Islands.

Another highlight is the Cactus Garden, where you will see an impressive collection of cacti and aloes with some outstanding specimens. One of them is curiously named Silla de la Suegra, which means the mother-in-law's chair.

The Butterfly House is the biggest in all Europe, with hundreds of exotic butterflies flying freely a truly unforgettable experience.

The **Aquarium** features a wide variety of tropical fishes, including the most important collection of coral fishes in Europe. Salt and freshwater fishes with the most amazing colours and shapes live in a recreated riverbed.

Another attraction is Primates Island, home to some White Handed Gibbons, whose natural habitats are the Malayan Peninsula and Burma and who have been successfully bred here, the first time in captivity.

All of this is set within more than 1,000 palm trees and 15,000 plants, representing an abundance of endemic and imported species.

Opening hours: Every day from 10.00 to 18.00 (admission until 5pm)

Exhibitions (daily):

Dolphins: 13.00 & 16.00
Parrots: 10.30, 11.30, 14.30, 15.30 & 16.30
Birds of Prey: 11.45 & 14.30
Exotic Birds: 14.00
Location: Barranco de Los Palmitos s/n, Maspalomas

Holiday World

The Holiday World leisure complex, popular with both locals and tourists, offers visitors a dizzying array of open-air amusement options.

The largest funfair on the Canary Islands features numerous exciting attractions such as a classic 27-metre-high Ferris wheel, a rollercoaster, dodgems, shooting stalls, seal and parrot shows and many more things to entertain the kids. It also comprises a leisure centre including a bowling alley, amusement arcades, a wellness centre with a health spa and a high-tech gym, various cafés and restaurants as well as two nightclubs (one of which is a salsa club), which already attract huge crowds at the weekends.

More for daytime use, you'll find a large park a five-minute walk away featuring a boating lake, children's playgrounds, pony riding, and a karting track... and these are just some of the attractions on offer.

Opening hours: Funfair: Monday to Friday, 18.00 to midnight, weekends 18.00 01.00.

Bowling, nightclubs and arcade centre: Monday to Friday, 10.00 02.00, weekends 10.00 03.00.

Location: Campo Internacional, in Maspalomas

Sioux City

Ride back in time and get the feel of the Wild Wild West. Meet mythical warriors like White Herb and cowboys such as Doc Holliday or get caught in a bank hold-up or a sudden shoot-out between cold-blooded cowpokes and the lawmen of Sioux City... This is a recreation of the American Wild West with gunfights, rustic barbecues, saloon gals, sheriffs and can-can girls... and to make the feel complete the air around you is filled with country & western music.

There are plenty of attractions to watch such as Duel until Death, Bank Robbery, Saloon Fight, Town-Square Hanging and Indian Rain Dance, along with Mexican acrobats performing stunts involving lassos, whips and knives... just to name some.

Covering a surface of 320.000 sq. meters, this park is a replica of a Wild West town with its typical houses, a church, a ranch, a bank and a saloon. And of course, where you see cowboys there also must be Indians... So don't miss the Indian reservation! For the kiddies (as if that wasn't already enough) there is a small zoo with some cute animals.

A fascinating attraction for both young and old... don't miss it!

Opening hours: 10.00 to 17.00 Tuesday to Saturday, closed on Mondays.

Fridays from 20.00 to midnight for BBQ and evening shows.

Location: Barranco del Águila, s/n. San Agustín, Maspalomas, Gran Canaria

Mundo Aborigen

Located in a setting of incomparable beauty overlooking the Barranco de Fataga, the biggest and most dramatic gorge on the island, you'll find Mundo Aborigen, a reconstruction of an ancient Canarian village devoted entirely to the Guanche way of life.

This park gives genuine insight into pre-Hispanic culture, with more than 100 human-size figures arranged in lifelike scenes and recorded domestic animal noises in the background to give the whole setting some realism. A marked trail leads through vivid descriptions of everything, from a butcher gutting a goat, a doctor holding a surgery, a farmer sowing a field to a convict being executed with a stone ...
To emphasise the most important aspects of Guanche culture, the site also houses a small archaeological museum has also been created on the site. It has been declared a place of historical, social and cultural interest by the local government.

Opening hours: everyday from 9.00 to 18.00

Location: Carretera de Fataga, Km 6 San Bartolomé de Tirajana

Cocodrilo Park

It all started when the Balser family was asked to take care of a few crocodiles... and now they have the largest collection in Europe. After the success of these first adoptions, the environmental protection police SEPRONA (Servicio de Protección de la Naturaleza de la Guardia Civil) has placed many animals in the Balser family's capable hands.

These animals including chimpanzees, various monkeys, birds, among many others usually arrive in very bad health due to being cruelly mistreated and confiscated from cargo ships, but they always recover under the professional care of the family.

This was the start of the Parque de los Cocodrilos, Gran Canaria's only zoological park. It was first opened to the public in 1988.

Since then the family have continuously added animals to the park by buying them from private individuals and circuses, and they are also breed freely in the park. The big family of Bengal tigers you'll see there, for example, were reared under the family's care.

Babu, one of the baboons handed to them in the past, was kept tied with the same chain around its waist until it was eight years old. It took two operations and months of treatment to get his health back and make him happy again.

About 300 crocodiles, species of tropical fishes, the Parrot Show on Treasure Island and a cacti garden number are amongst the attractions you'll see in this unusual animal park.

What's more, your entrance fees directly support the upkeep of this ever-growing park and the salaries for its professional and caring staff.

Opening hours: Sunday to Friday from 10.00 to 17.00 (last admission at 16.00)

Location: Carretera Gral Los Coralillos - Agüimes

Cactualdea Park (Cactus Park)

Tourists flock to Cactualdea, in the west of the island. A Cactus Park with thousands of cacti imported from countries like Mexico, Madagascar, Guatemala and Bolivia, it's set between palms, dragon trees and aloe.

There's also a Guanche Cave and a traditional restaurant serving typical Canarian dishes with an impressive wine cellar. Another place of interest is a large amphitheatre used for lucha canaria (Canarian wrestling) bouts.

Opening hours: everyday from 10.00 to 18.00 (summer) and 10.00 to 17.00 (winter)

Location: Ctra. De Mogán a San Nicolás de Tolentino, s/n. Ctra. del Hoyo-Tocodoman

Pueblo Canario (Canarian Village), Parque Doramas

One of the main attractions in Las Palmas is the Pueblo Canario (Canarian Village), located within the Parque Doramas. In the 1930s, the brothers Néstor and Miguel Martín-Fernández de la Torre conceived the idea of building the Pueblo Canario as a way of promoting increased interest in local culture and traditions.

Nowadays, visitors can stroll past the houses of a typical Canarian village and admire the famous wooden carved balconies, turrets of the traditional architecture. Twice a week, the main square doubles up as a stage for folk groups who perform lively dances to the sounds of local songs; enjoy the show while you sample some delicious Canarian delicacies at the Bodegón Canario, washed down with generous supplies of local wine, of course!

The Museo Néstor, mainly exhibits the works of Symbolist artist Néstor Martín-Fernández de la Torre and there are also regular cultural activities programmed such as concerts and conferences.
A pretty and very relaxed place in the heart of a big city, the Pueblo Canario is well worth a visit.
Opening hours: Tuesday Saturday 10.00 to 20.00 hrs Sunday 10.30 to 14.30 hrs
Location: Parque Doramas City of Las Palmas

Sport

Gran Canaria's fantastic weather makes it a firm favourite among sporty people who enjoy taking part in the huge range of activities the island has to offer... especially water sports. Maybe you like to sail? Or windsurf? Or go fishing? Here at Spain-Grancanaria, we have put together some information on the main sports available to whet your appetite. Read on...

Deep sea fishing

If you like an adrenaline rush then you'll love big-game fishing!

With the lure of some of the world's most exciting species such as barracuda, tuna, marlin and wahoo, Gran Canaria offers sports fishermen a real challenge. Fishing trips can be organised at the principal charter marinas located at Las Palmas (Santa Catalina pier), Pasito Blanco and Puerto Rico.

Diving

The warm, crystal clear waters found around Gran Canaria make scuba diving a popular pastime for holidaymakers. The seabed is colourful and the marine life varied. Divers will encounter rays, groupers, barracudas, turtles, tropical fish and occasionally sharks. There are many diving schools to choose from here, but make sure they are certified and offer all safety requirements; the best bet is to ask for professional schools at your hotel's reception.

Sailing

If you have salt-water in your veins look for marinas, local sailing clubs and federations where you may be able to rent yachts or catamarans for day excursions or longer trips. In Las Palmas search for the Federación de Vela, the Puerto Deportivo or the Real Club Náutico de Gran Canaria. In Maspalomas head to the Catamaran Club, the Maspalomas Yacht Club or the Puerto Deportivo de Mogán.

Water-skiing

There are many schools in different locations; too numerous to list, most tourist beaches offer water-skiing, jet-skiing and parasailing facilities.

Windsurfing

This is one of the most popular sports and is practiced off many beaches. It does not matter where you are; there always seems to be enough breeze to head out with your board and sail.

There are many great places for windsurfing in Gran Canaria such as: Playa de las Canteras (Las Palmas), Dunkerbeck F2 Windsurfing School or Passat School (both in Maspalomas), and Joaquín Blanco, a sailing school in Puerto Rico.

Hiking

Away from the coast there are plenty of countryside landscapes to explore. Gran Canaria has a rugged interior and lots of Caminos Reales (royal pathways), which are ancient roads dating back to Guanche times. Many of them have been maintained and are used by hikers, providing a wonderful opportunity to see the island from a new perspective.

Canarian Wrestling

Canarian wrestling (Lucha Canaria) is a popular sport watched by people throughout the islands. The basic objective of this sport is to throw the opponent to the ground, in teams usually consisting of 12 wrestlers. Some of the inter-island competitions, where teams from all over the Canaries play each other, are shown on Canarian TV. Matches are sometimes held on Playa de las Canteras in Las Palmas.

Water Sports

The mild, as opposed to wild, weather conditions all year round make Gran Canaria the perfect destination for those looking for plenty of fun in the sea. Sea temperatures rarely drop below 18ºC in winter, the average temperature for the rest of the year being around 23°C.

Sailing

Gran Canaria is a sailor's dream, especially from April to October. The sailing centres can be found in Las Palmas, where the annual Atlantic Rally for Cruisers (ARC) departs from, and on the south coast, specifically Puerto Rico, Pasito Blanco, Arguineguín and Puerto Mogán. In these ports, a number of schools offer equipment hire and tuition. Gran Canaria boasts some of the best practicing conditions worldwide with local sailing clubs producing several Olympic champions. Head to any resort by the sea and you will easily find a school or company providing you with what you need to start sailing.

Windsurfing

Gran Canaria is considered one of the best places in the world for windsurfing. You can windsurf all along the coast from the east to the south, but there're also very good conditions at Playa de las Canteras in Las Palmas and at Gáldar in the north west.

If you want to see the top windsurfers in action, though, head to Pozo Izquierdo, where winds can reach speeds of up to 60 kmph, and to Playa de Vargas, one of the venues of the PWA Wave Classic Grand Prix.

If you're just starting this sport, though, it's best you stick to sheltered harbours such as Puerto Rico and Puerto de Mogán.

Bodyboarding and Surfing

You can best enjoy these water sports on the north coast, between Las

Palmas and Gáldar. Constant on-shore winds provide surfers with ideal conditions and waves that can be up to 5 metres high. Little wonder then that Gran Canaria has been dubbed the European Hawaii.

There are also good conditions on the east coast, around Arinaga and in the south between Playa del Inglés and Maspalomas.

If you don't want to bring your own board, there are several places in Gran Canaria where you can hire the necessary equipment.

Scuba Diving

The underwater world truly fascinates in Gran Canaria, with subtropical fishes, shipwrecks and caves representing some of the beauties you'll see on your trip down under.

Finding a fully certified diving school in one of the major seaside resorts will not be a problem. Most of them offer beginner and advanced courses for more experienced divers, and also rent out diving equipment. Beginners should always start in sheltered harbours first before trying the open sea.

When diving in Gran Canaria, you shouldn't miss visiting the marine reserve of El Cabrón off the east coast at Playa del Cabrón (wow factor 30), Pasito Blanco with its ideal conditions for underwater photography and two wrecks to explore for experienced divers.

There's also the fascinating diving sites of La Isleta in the north east and Sardina de Norte in the north west of the island.

Deep-sea Fishing

If you are into big-game fishing, this is the place to come especially during the main season from May to September. But Gran Canaria also provides ample opportunities to bottom-fish.

The major resorts in Gran Canaria house several companies offering deep-sea fishing, but the best harbours to set out from for this sport are Puerto de Mogán, Pasito Blanco and Puerto Rico - Puerto Rico's 50+ deep-sea fishing world records speak for themselves. The main species to be found off the coast in these regions include several varieties of tuna and marlin, swordfish and, occasionally, sharks.

Marine Excursions

Cruises along the coasts, enjoy underwater excursions in a glass-bottom boat, dolphin and whale watching, on half-day or full-day tours... there's a wide range of offers available at most of the major tourist resorts. You'll find the biggest choice in places like Puerto Rico or Puerto de Mogán, where several companies specialise in off-shore leisure trips. Don't rush into a decision, keep looking and compare prices and services. You'll see that some offer more for a lower price, but the majority will provide you with a good quality service.

Parascending, Jet & Water Skiing

The major resorts in the south offer parascending, jet-skiing, water-skiing, speedboat trips and other adrenalin-pumping activities. You can also hire the ever-popular banana boats, pedal boats and sea kayaks –the perfect excuse for getting out on the water with your children.

Golf in Gran Canaria

Ideal climatic conditions make Gran Canaria a perfect golfing destination, with the possibility of practicing your favourite sport 365 days a year. An added bonus is that most of the golf courses on the island are new, which means you'll find modern courses conceived with the most demanding players very much in mind.

There are currently 8 golf courses in Gran Canaria each and every one built by the most prestigious of international golf-course designers. Experts rate many of these courses as some of the best in Spain.

Real Club de Golf de Las Palmas:

Founded by British expatriates in 1891, the Real Club de Golf de Las Palmas is actually the oldest golf course in all Spain. Situated south of the Pico de Bandama, this course boasts wonderful views over Caldera de Bandama, a spectacular volcanic crater.

Designed by Mackenzie Ross, this is a par-71, 18-hole course, with two putting greens, practice tee, pitching green, instructors, pro-shop, club hire service, restaurant and an excellent wine cellar. There are also two tennis courts, a horse-riding area and a swimming pool.

Location: Carretera de Bandama s/n 35380 Santa Brígida

Las Palmeras Golf:

Designed by Antonio García Garrido, this par-54, 18-hole course opened in 2006. Offering a convenient city-centre location, Las Palmeras enjoys views over Canteras beach and the surging Atlantic.

Rounding off the golfing facilities are a 1000m2 putting green and a sizeable chipping area too. The children's area and nursery will come in handy for those with kids. There's also a snack bar, restaurant and terrace.

Location: Avenida Doctor Alfonso Chiscano Díaz s/n Las Palmas

El Cortijo de Campo:

This course has been the venue for important international championships, as well as the centre for the Peugeot Oki Tour and the Professional Senior and Women's Spanish Championships. Designed by Blake Stirling (head designer of Pete Dye) and Marco Martín, this par-72, 18-hole course features fast greens and, with up to six tees per hole, offers great variety and sufficient difficulty. It also boasts six lakes and more than 600 century-old palm trees surrounding them. Other facilities include a golf school, practice course, chipping green, putting green and practice bunker, as well as a service for the hire of carts, bags and clubs.

Location: Autopista del Sur G.C. 1 / Km 6,4 - Telde

Oasis Golf:

Experts consider this 18-hole, par-54 course, a miniaturised replica of famous American courses, to be one of the best in the world. Several obstacles, such as spectacular lakes and sand bunkers, form a marvellous contrast to the green lushness of this course. As the only floodlit course in Gran Canaria, Oasis Golf encourages visiting golfers to play at night too when temperatures are especially in summer times more bearable. It also houses a pro-shop, restaurant, bag and club hire, as well as a children's nursery.

Location: Autopista del Sur G.C. 1 / Km 6,4 - Telde

Maspalomas Golf:

When Mackenzie Ross came to designing this course, he took into account the surrounding dunes. As a result, Maspalomas Golf offers an extremely long and flat course with lengthy, wide lanes. Even on the hottest days, the proximity of the sea and the mild breezes cooled by the trade winds, make a visit to this course an unforgettable experience.

This 18-hole, par-73 course plays host to a number of prestigious international competitions, and boasts a practice green, driving range, instructors, facilities for the hire of carts, bags and clubs, shop, restaurant and snack bars.
Location: Avda. Touroperador Neckermann - Maspalomas

Salobre Golf & Resort:
You'll find Salobre Golf, one of the newest golf clubs in Gran Canaria, set in a magnificent scenery with ravines and volcanic landscapes typical of the south of the island. Indeed, the lush greenery of the course forms a strong contrast to its surroundings.

Designed by Roland Fauré, the interesting and demanding par-71, 18-hole Salobre Sur course covers a length of 6 km. The trickier Salobre Norte, also known as the Beast Course and designed by Ron Kirby, likewise features 18 holes but is par-72. This complex's facilities include a golf school, practice area, driving range, putting green, club hire, hydro-massage, pro-shop and restaurant with terrace.
Location: Autopista Gran Canaria 1 / Km 53 - Urbanización El Salobre Maspalomas

Anfi Tauro Golf:

You'll find Anfi Tauro Golf in the municipality of Mogán, on the south side of the island. Featuring a 9-hole, par 27 pitch-and-putt course, opened in 2001, and a newer 18-hole par-72 course, this club is set in stunning surroundings. Boasting spectacular lakes of crystal-clear water and a wide variety of plants and flowers, it also affords magnificent views of the mountains. Apart from a putting green and a practice area, there's a cafeteria and driving range.

Location: Barranco del Lechugal, Valle de Tauro s/n Mogán

Meloneras Golf:

This beautiful golf course runs alongside the Meloneras Bay in the south of the island and was designed by Ron Kirby. Featuring an 18-hole, par-71 course with 9 holes offering stunning mountain views and the other 9 look over the ocean. The design of the course is very attractive with the holes starting off easy then steadily becoming more difficult. Attention to detail is a big thing for Meloneras Golf even the golf carts come equipped with GPS!

Location: Autopista GC 500, s/n, Meloneras

Air Sports

Skydiving, Parachuting, Hang-gliding, Paragliding and Flying

If you're more of the adventurous type and love the feel of freedom and weightlessness, there are plenty of companies on the island, which offer these exhilarating sports, very often including courses for beginners as well as the more advanced.

For flying, parachuting, hang-gliding or paragliding contact either the Club de Parapente Las Palmas or the Club Deportivo Siroco, both in Las Palmas, or the Paraclub Gran Canaria in the south.

For skydiving a 20-minute flight over the Maspalomas dunes and a jump in tandem with an instructor contact Skydive Gran Canaria (this company operates from the far end of the Paseo Marítimo, where the dunes begin).

Cycling

The island's mountainous terrain, combined with one of the best all-year- round climates in the world, creates ideal conditions for mountain biking and cycling. These attributes attract many race teams to Gran Canaria for their winter training or bicycle tourists, who bring their own bike with them to explore the natural beauties of the island while practicing their favourite sport.

There are of course several places, where you can rent a bike and do your own bicycle tourism on a broad network of available routes, but there are also many leisure companies providing guided bicycle tours, which often include a picnic lunch in the outing.

Bicycles also offer an excellent means of transport and many tourists use touring bikes to do their shopping or to reach distant places and beaches to escape from the crowds.

However, be aware that, given the nature of the terrain, the steep hills, the narrow and winding roads as well as lots of car traffic, cycling on the island requires intense concentration. Don't take any unnecessary risks either.

Nightlife

Nightlife in Gran Canaria is lively, noisy and fun. It starts late and goes on all night with most bars opening until 02.00 and discos and clubs usually until 06.00. Very little happens before midnight.

Like anywhere else, discos, clubs and bars fall in and out of favour very rapidly, so things may be changed when you come to Gran Canaria. But if you are staying in Las Palmas, the place to go is Plaza de España in the Mesa y Lopéz district, which is always lively until early morning. Here, you will find the old Heineken, where many locals start their evening.

Elsewhere there's Cuasquías, a popular venue for free live music, Nowanda Café Club, recommended for jazz aficionados and the Mojo

Club, next to the Auditorio Alfredo Kraus, a good place to take in enthusiastic DJ sets.

And even more is going on all along the south coast. It's impossible to get bored in a place where nobody seems to sleep, except at siesta time that is. There are hundreds of bars, clubs and discos catering for a wide range of tastes, especially in Playa del Inglés, Maspalomas and Meloneras. Just head for the big shopping centres and choose what's best for you. On your way to the main nightlife areas, you'll always encounter people on the street handing out flyers and encouraging you to visit their bar/disco/club.

In Playa del Inglés look out for the Yumbo (famous for its gay scene), Kasbah (where the young and beautiful meet) and Plaza, and dance along to the latest international music hits. And in July 2010 the infamous Pacha opened its doors in Playa del Inglés.

If you prefer a quieter atmosphere and you'd like to try your luck, there are two casinos in Gran Canaria, the Casino Las Palmas situated inside the Hotel Santa Catalina in the city of Las Palmas, and the Gran Canaria Casino, which you'll find in the Hotel Meliá Tamarindos in San Agustín.

And don't forget Meloneras with its stylish and contemporary bars and cafés. There are plenty of places to chill out and watch the sunset while enjoying your favourite tipple.

Culture

An important landmark for the cultural development of the Canaries was the incorporation of the islands into the Castilian Crown at the end of the 15th century. This marked the beginning of Hispanic culture and tradition spreading across all the islands of the archipelago.

Gran Canaria boasts several interesting museums and culture centres. The main highlights include the Museo Elder de la Ciencia y la Tecnología (Science and Technology Museum) and the Casa de Colón (Christopher Columbus House), as well as the Centro Atlántico de Arte Moderno (Atlantic Centre of Modern Art). All of these are great places to visit and can be found in the city of Las Palmas itself.

After the subjugation by the Spaniards, Gran Canaria became a famous port of call for travellers and many of them settled with their families on this beautiful island, bringing with them their own cultures and traditions.

Gran Canaria's society has always been open to influences from beyond the seas, which has enriched the island with visiting cultures over the years. However, it has always been important for the island to preserve its ancient traditions and to keep its original identity alive. Due to its long history, this cosmopolitan island has become a synonym for cultural blending with a rich archaeological, architectural, ethnographic and artistic heritage a rare quality for a place as small as Gran Canaria.

The Canarios like to celebrate festivals, be it of religious or cultural nature, and there is always something going on somewhere on the island. Internationally-renowned festivals include the International Film Festival of Las Palmas, the Festival de Música de Canarias (Canarian Classical Music Festival) and the Festival de Ópera. Other events such as the WOMAD (World of Music, Arts and Dance) and the Festival de Teatro y Danza de Las Palmas de Gran Canaria (Theatre and Dance Festival) bring still more influences from the international cultural panorama to this magnificent island.

The Island Cultural Centre

The neighbourhood of Vegueta in Las Palmas is the place to be if you are interested in culture, whether that is visiting museums, photography exhibitions or places of historical interest.

The art scene is alive and well here; stunning architecture and the character of its atmosphere enhance the artistic feel of this vibrant quarter. From shops and galleries to museums, Vegueta will delight, amaze and satisfy your cultural interests.

Traditional works and artists are well represented in the Canaries as are their contemporary counterparts. The former 'Island Cultural Centre' did a great job promoting the island's work and since it closed, visitors are encouraged to explore the gems of Vegueta instead.

For avant-garde and ethnic exhibitions, head to the Centro Atlántico de Arte Moderno (CAAM), which also displays a permanent exhibition of Canarian artwork.

If pre-Hispanic is what you are looking for, the largest collection of these artefacts (including mummies and other remains from Guanche times) dating from 500 BC to the 15th century, can be found at the Museo Canario in Vegueta.

The Canaries are really a wealth of riches for those of you interested in history. Vegueta also boasts the Casa de Colón, named so because Christopher Columbus is believed to have stayed in the building while he was having one of his ships repaired.

For theatre, opera, ballet and concerts you can head to Teatro Pérez Galdós. The impressive Auditorio Alfredo Kraus, close to Playa de las Canteras, is home to the International Film Festival of Las Palmas de Gran Canaria, the Canary Islands Music Festival and the Philharmonic Orchestra of Gran Canaria.

All hotel receptions will be able to give you in-depth information and programmes of forthcoming events during your stay so that you can make the most of your visit to this beautiful location.

Museums

During your stay, you might have the opportunity to visit some of Gran Canaria's museums that will allow you to discover its rich historical past and to better understand local culture. Casa de Colón is believed to have been the place where Christopher Columbus stayed in 1492 and shows its visitors aspects of the old local architecture.

But modernity is also just around the corner, behind the traditional façade of Centro Atlántico de Arte Moderno, where you will most certainly be surprised by the architectural contrast when you step into the building. Another place of interest is Pueblo Canario, where you will get a global perspective of what a typical Canarian village looks like and also have the chance to see local handicraft and hear Canarian music. So whether you prefer something old or something new, Gran Canaria is the right choice for you!

Casa de Colón (Columbus House)

The Casa de Colón is one of Las Palmas most attractive buildings with ornate doorways, beautiful latticed balconies, large courtyards and carved wooden ceilings, representing numerous aspects of the island's architecture. This palace was the residence of the first governors of the island and it is claimed that Christopher Columbus stayed there in 1492 while one of his ships was repaired, hence the name Casa de Colón (Columbus House).

This charming building was rebuilt in 1777 and since 1952 has housed a museum comprising 13 permanent exhibition rooms, a library and study centre as well as several spaces reserved for temporary activities, such as lectures, seminars and exhibitions. On display are pre-Columbian artefacts, ship models, a replica of a cabin of La Niña, one ship of Columbus' fleet, navigation instruments, nautical maps and charts, paintings as well as many other artefacts related to voyages made by the famous navigator and the history of the Canaries and their relationship with the Americas.

This house was also the birthplace of the celebrated opera tenor, Alfredo Kraus (1927-99). Of more interest to younger visits will be the pair of parrots in the courtyard, especially as they're particularly talkative.

Opening hours:
Monday to Saturday 10.00 to 18.00 - Sundays and Public holidays 10.00 to 15.00 (Closed: January 1st and 6th, May 1st, December 24th, 25th and 31st). Entry: 4€

In the Calle de los Balcones, a cobbled street off the Plaza del Pilar and running parallel to the sea, you'll encounter a modest-looking building that in contrast to its 18th century façade houses the futuristic Centro Atlántico de Arte Moderno (Altantic Modern Art Centre).

Centro Atlántico de Arte Moderno
Since its inauguration in 1989 the Centro Atlántico de Arte Moderno (CAAM) has become a major reference in the cultural and educational life of the islanders. Concealed behind a traditional façade, formerly belonging to a hotel, this centre is definitely worth visiting especially because of its spectacular interior design with white walls, marble stairs and acres of glass.

CAAM organises exhibitions, mainly of avant-garde art, and it has its own collection of works created by artists who had a substantial influence on the shaping of 20th-century Canarian art.

One other main objective of this Atlantic Modern Art Centre is to show the connection of Canarian art with that from Africa, the Americas and Europe, as the culture of the archipelago is largely determined by the influence of these three continents.

CAAM also provides a venue for courses, lectures and seminars, allowing the visitors to study the exhibitions in depth and from different perspectives.

Opening hours:
Tuesday Saturday 10:00 to 21:00 Sundays 10:00 to 14:00 Closed on Mondays and bank holidays. Free entry.

Our tip:
There is a guided tour available from Tuesdays Sunday from 10:00 to 21:00 but advanced booking is required and there needs to be a minimum of 5 people.

Museo Canario

Founded in 1879 by a small group of members of the local bourgeoisie, the Museo Canario houses the Canary Islands' largest collection of pre-Hispanic objects from the period of 500 B.C. until the 15th century.

Head of this private initiative aiming to preserve, research and exhibit the archaeological and documentary collections of the museum was Doctor Gregorio Chil y Naranjo who left the building and all the scientific documents to the private foundation managing this museum in his will.

Spread over 11 rooms, you'll find a very eclectic permanent exhibition with statuettes of gods, jewellery, pottery, tools, mummies, skeletons and many other artefacts related to the life of the Guanches, the aborigines of the Canaries. The displays also include scale models of Guanche dwellings and a replica of the Cueva Pintada at Gáldar. Endowed with an extensive library, a periodicals' library and an archive specialised in Canarian matters, this museum also offers its services to researchers, students and the general public.

Opening hours:

- Museum, Temporary Exhibitions and Shop:

Monday Friday 10.00 to 20.00

Saturdays and Sundays 10.00 to 14.00

- Library, Periodicals' Library and Archive:

Monday Friday 10.00 to 20.00 closed on bank holidays

Note:

The Museo Canario boasts the world's largest collection of Cro-

Magnon skulls and displays Guanche implements and a collection of pottery.

Casa Museo de Pérez Galdós

The birthplace of Benito Pérez Galdós (1843 1920), the most distinguished writer from the Canary Islands, was turned into a museum commemorating the author's life and work. This three-storey building which the author continued to live in until 1862, is a fine example of 18th century Canarian architecture, built around a small patio adorned with a statue of the writer.

The Casa Museo de Pérez Galdós, which opened in 1964, still boasts the original interior decoration and displays objects associated with the writer's life; portraits and items from his houses in Madrid and Santander, many of which he designed and made himself, as well as photographs of many actors who appeared in his plays.

A library contains original works and translations, correspondence, meeting minutes and dissertations from this greatly-revered author.

Opening hours:
Monday Friday 10 :00 to 14 :00 hrs and 16 :00 to 20 :00
Saturday & Sunday 10 :00 to 14 :00
Our tip:

Free to enter, this museum also offers guided tours.

Note:

The museum is currently closed for refurbishment.

Pueblo Canario, Museo Néstor

Another visitor attraction of the Parque Doramas is the Pueblo Canario (Canarian Village), a complex of traditionally-built houses forming a typical Canarian village with gates, turrets and an atrium.

Designed in the 1930s by the brothers Néstor and Miguel Fernández de la Torre to interest tourists in native culture, this village boasts a large central square, surrounded by shops selling local handicrafts, where regular shows of Canarian music and dance take place.

The Museo Néstor, dedicated to life and works of the better known of the two brothers, is also part of this complex. Opened in 1956, this museum exhibits a multitude of works of this artist, considered one of Spain's principal symbolist painters. They include both portraits and landscapes, highlights of which are eight murals illustrating his Poema del Mar.

Opening hours of the museum:

Tuesday Saturday 10.00 to 20.00

Sunday 10.30 to 14.30

Eating Out

Canarian Food

The cuisine of the Canary Islands combines traditional Spanish recipes with African and Latin-American influences. Some recipes have been imported from the Spanish mainland, but many original flavours can be found in the Canarian specialities. You will find Spanish food on the menu of many restaurants in the resorts and hotels, as well as a wide variety of international food. It is well worth searching for genuine local cuisine - your taste buds will not be disappointed!

The basis of the typical local cuisine is a variety of vegetables, fruit and fish. Meat usually features as part of a stew and steaks are mostly imported from mainland Spain or South America. Thanks to Gran Canaria's wonderful Climate, colourful local markets in every town offer an abundance of seasonal produce that is fresh and inexpensive. Sample locally-made specialities, including chorizo, goat's cheese and honey.

A stone-ground flour called gofio, made from toasted barley, maize and wheat, forms an essential part of the Canarian diet. It is used to thicken soups and sauces and is often stirred into children's milk as it is rich in protein, fibre, minerals and vitamins. Gofio also forms the basis of two particularly scrumptious local desserts, helado de gofio (gofio ice cream) and mus de gofio (gofio mousse).

Also definitely worth trying are papas arrugadas (wrinkled potatoes), otherwise known as Canarian potatoes. This dish consists of small, new potatoes boiled with their jackets on in salty water, but their real flavour comes from the accompanying mojos (sauces). Using olive oil as a base, various herbs and spices are added to create a piquant green, red, or orange-coloured sauce.

If you like fish, you will be in paradise in Gran Canaria. Among the most typical regional recipes are caldo de pescado (fish soup) and vieja sancochada (sea-bream casserole). Sancocho Canario is served during fiestas and on Sundays a special stew made from salted cod and sweet potato. Freshly grilled sardines are also popular, particularly in Sardina de Norte, a town tucked away on Gran Canaria's northern coast.

Some local restaurants even have their own fishing boats which go out daily to catch fresh crab, lobsters and fish. These then go straight onto the menu for visitors to savour and enjoy!

The most typical dessert is bienmesabe (literally: 'it tastes good to me'), a combination of ground almonds, lemon rind, sugar and eggs. Besides that, you have a wide choice of tropical fruits, like mango, avocado and papaya. Huevos mole is another popular pudding, made from egg yolks beaten with sugar syrup and cinnamon. Also look out for the marzipan pralines from Tejeda and the sponges and meringues from Moya, which are the very definition of 'moreish'.

Try the delicious Ron Miel (honey Rum), which is considered a local delicacy and can be found in market stalls, shops and behind the bar of most restaurants. Most people drink it straight or with a little ice, while others like to add it to coffee. A wide selection of Spanish wines and beers is also served all over the island.

Note:

The tradition of having tapas before meals is one of the most important Spanish contributions to the world of gastronomy. A tapa is a small, light mini-serving of a traditional recipe that Spaniards have either before lunch or dinner, always with a glass of wine or beer. The tapas tradition is a perfect excuse to have one or two drinks before the actual meal! The word 'tapa' comes from an old medieval tradition where wine was served with a small piece of ham that acted as a lid to cover the drink. Hence the word 'tapa', which literally means 'lid' in Spanish. Tapas can be presented in several ways - as a pincho (on a toothpick), as a small portion of a particular dish or as a canapé. Bear in mind, that in Gran Canaria, tapas are known as enyesques.

Shopping

Shopping in Gran Canaria

With the introduction of the Euro, items which used to be considerably cheaper in Gran Canaria became more expensive. But as the Canary Islands managed to maintain their status of a free trade zone with lower import tax and VAT rates, despite Spain's membership of the EU, some consumer goods like alcohol, tobacco, perfume, jewellery, clothing and electronic goods can still be bought cheaper at duty-free shops in Las Palmas and the south coast resorts.

Yet, be aware that unlike everywhere else in the European Union there are strict limits for goods being exported for personal use to other European Union countries. Therefore, you're only allowed to return with 1 litre of spirits, 2 litres of wine and 200 cigarettes (or 50 cigars).

Popular souvenirs include local handicrafts like baskets made out of banana leaves, pottery, embroidery, felt hats and miniature versions of the famous Canary wooden balconies. For the best quality at reasonable prices look for the outlets of FEDAC Fundación Para la Etnografía y el Desarrollo de la Artesanía Canaria in Las Palmas and Playa del Inglés and at the weekly markets taking place in several towns around the island.

The city of Las Palmas is without doubt Gran Canaria's largest commercial centre. Here, you'll find all the major chain and franchise stores, both Spanish and international. The city's biggest shopping centres are Las Arenas (near the Auditorio Alfredo Kraus), La Ballena (in the north of the city), the traditional Avenida Mesa y López (near Santa Catalina Park), also known as 'zona comercial', where there are two branches of the famous El Corte Inglés chain, and the Calle Mayor de Triana, in the heart of the old Triana district, with a medley of shops, ranging from tiny fabric stores to old-fashioned tobacconists and international franchise outlets. El Muelle, at the Muelle Santa Catalina, is a light, bright shopping mall with a wide range of shops, restaurants, cafés, a cinema and discos.

2008 brought the opening of the eye-catching Las Terrazas, located in Jinamar between Las Palmas and the airport. Despite the credit crunch, 20,000 people visited on its opening day. Besides the sea, it offers ample parking and many outlets with discounts of up to 70% on labels such as Calvin Klein, Levi's and Pepe Jeans. There are many cafés and restaurants too, including one selling all their sandwiches for a bargain 1 Euro.

The shopping centres of Playa del Inglés of which the best known are probably Yumbo and Kasbah and the biggest is Cita stay busy seven days a week, but the emphasis here is on price rather than quality. These shopping centres are usually huge buildings, where you can find almost everything clothes, electronic goods, jewellery, perfumes as well as lots of animated bars, restaurants and clubs. The supermarkets all along the south coast also sell a wide range of local and imported food and drink.

And the new resort of Meloneras offers a great shopping experience. Here you'll find loads of high end stores like Ralph Lauren and Lacoste. This is a place for labels as well as independent boutiques. The start of Meloneras is marked by the lighthouse and from here all the way along the promenade there is a wealth of shops in between the bars, cafes and restaurants. This resort is best for up-market goods rather than the typical tourist gifts you'll find elsewhere. If you come to Meloneras specifically to shop then make sure you bring lots of cash. High quality equals expense. Enjoy.

Others Things to Do

Explore Vegueta, the old town of Las Palmas

Vegueta is the name given to the old town part of Las Palmas, the capital city of Gran Canaria. A visit here will transport you back in time as it has remained relatively unchanged since Columbus visited in the late 1400s, so you can get a real taste of the island's history while you're here.

Strolling around the district's narrow, cobbled streets with its historical architecture and traditional wooden balconies, you'll discover a number of fascinating sights and attractions to explore. Some of the most popular include the Casa de Colon mansion, the popular Museo Canario museum, the town hall, the Centro Atlantico de Arte Moderno gallery and the impressive Catedral de Santa Ana that dominates the landscape.

You can also browse the markets and many shops in the area or even head across the road to the much more modern Triana shopping district if you fancy a bigger spree. But after all that exploring, you'll be in need of refuelling. Lucky for you, you'll find some excellent outdoor terraces all around Vegueta for you to grab a refreshing drink and a tasty bite to eat.

Bandama Caldera

If you're a nature lover and enjoy nothing more than getting out and exploring your surroundings while on holiday, then seeing Gran Canaria's Caldera de Bandama is an absolute must. Part of the island's

Tafia Protected Landscape, it's a fascinating volcanic crater and a point of geological interest.

The crater stands at 569m above sea level; it's about 1,000m wide and about 200m deep. Inside, you'll find volcanic ash of all different shades, as well as ancient rock carvings and a number of different botanic species; all native to the Canary Islands.

It's definitely worth the trip up here, even if it's just to take in the incredible panoramic views from the top. The peak has an observation deck and on a really clear day, you might even be able to see as far as the island of Fuerteventura.

The crater is located at the meeting point of Las Palmas de Gran Canaria, Telde and Santa Brigida.

Hike to the impressive Roque Nublo

Standing proud at 80 metres tall, Roque Nublo is an icon of Gran Canaria and actually marks the centre of the island. Looking at photos, you'd be forgiven for thinking that the rock is something that only mountaineers or the most experienced of explorers can visit, but it's actually easily accessible for all to see.

The name itself translates as 'Cloud Rock' for the simple reason that it often disappears into the clouds. But chances are you'll still get a clear view from the top once you're up there. You'll be surprised at just how big the rock is once you're stood in front of it, but you can't actually walk around it as it's perched right on the edge of the mountainside. You'd have to be a pretty daring and experienced climber to give that a go.

If you like the sound of exploring Roque Nublo for yourself, you're in luck as it's really easy to get to. If you have a hire car, you can park in the La Goleta car park, which is on the road in between San Bartolome de Tirajana and Tejed. From there you can follow the fairly steep track which takes you to the top in about 15 minutes. Then just take a moment to absorb the stunning panoramic views in front of you.

Paddle surfing in Gran Canaria

You can't go to Gran Canaria without spending some time soaking up the year-round sun on the island's beautiful, golden beaches. But maybe you crave something a little more than just lounging on the sand? The Canary Islands are perfect for trying your hand at different water sports and the beaches of Gran Canaria are home to a whole variety of activities for you to choose from.

A really fun way to spend your day at the beach is to get out and experience paddle surfing. If you're not sure what that is, it combines surfing and rowing, where you stand up on the surf board and gently glide along the water surface using an oar. It's perfect for those who love the water, but perhaps aren't so keen on the more adrenaline-fuelled water sports. It's also ideal for those days when the water's a bit too calm to catch any waves.

There are lots of places where you can try paddle surfing in Gran Canaria, including Playa del Inglés and Las Palmas de Gran Canaria, which have a number of dedicated paddle surfing schools. So why not give it a go on your next holiday?

Spend the day at Palmitos Park

Palmitos Park is an absolute must when on holiday in Gran Canaria. It's one of the most popular attractions on the island, so much so that it's currently ranked the number two thing to do out of over 220 attractions, according to people on TripAdvisor.

The park is a 49 acre botanical garden which features over 1,500 exotic birds of over 230 different species. It's a great day out for the whole family as you can explore the subtropical park, seeing how many of the birds you can spot flying freely, as well as taking in the incredible views as you go.

There are many other attractions to experience throughout the park, besides the giant aviary. Palmitos Park is home to the biggest butterfly house in all of Europe and also gives you the opportunity to see monkeys, crocodiles, birds of prey, an aquarium, an orchid house, hummingbirds and even get up close and personal with their four resident dolphins.

In July 2007, the park had to close for a year following some devastating forest fires, but reopened again the following August. There's now a whole new section of the park that shares information about the fire, which is worth visiting while you're there.

After a fun-filled day making your way around the entire park, be sure to visit the on-site souvenir shop to take home a memento of your visit.

Spend the day exploring the Jardin Canario

The Jardin Canario is a unique and vast botanical paradise that features every type of vegetation and plant that you can expect to find on the Canary Islands. It's the biggest botanical garden in all of Spain and is the perfect place to spend a few hours if you maybe need a break from the beach.

You can walk around all the many different sections and see all kinds of exotic and unusual plant life that you may never have even heard of or seen before; everything from brightly coloured flowers to odd-shaped cactus plants. The majority of people enter via the lower levels of the garden, which is ideal for those with pushchairs, wheelchairs or mobility issues. But it's also possible to wander deeper into the gardens by exploring the different cliff paths that lead you to higher, less visited levels. There are great views from up there too.

Other key parts to check out include the waterfall, the cactus garden and the huge array of palm trees. There's a small restaurant at the Jardin Canario, should you fancy a bite to eat. But you could always take your own food with you and enjoy a picnic amongst your beautiful surroundings.

Visit the historic Catedral de Santa Ana

Head to the island's capital, Las Palmas, and right in the heart of the old town you'll find the Catedral de Santa Ana dominating the landscape. This impressive cathedral is the very first church of all the Canary Islands, having been ordered to be built following the conquering of Gran Canaria in 1478.

Construction began on the cathedral in 1500, but wasn't completed until nearly four centuries later. As you can imagine, this means that there were several different designers and artists working on the build, so you can see a number of different architectural styles throughout. The three main ones being Gothic, Renaissance and Neoclassical.

There is a small charge for adults entering the twin-towered cathedral, but it's well worth a look around. Inside you'll find chapels containing incredible sculptures and pieces of art. Then there's also the Museo Diocesano de Arte Sacro, or Sacred Art Museum, located in the Patio de los Naranjos in the cathedral's south wing. The museum holds a number of fascinating artefacts, paintings and more sculptures for you to learn about.

As well as the captivating architecture and exhibits, a visit to the Catedral de Santa Ana wouldn't be complete without taking the lift up the south tower to take in the excellent panoramic views of the city and the harbour from the top.

What's On and Lively
What's on in Gran Canaria

Gran Canaria has become a cosmopolitan island with numerous cultural events throughout the year, including international music, dance, theatre and cinema festivals and the many carnival celebrations. Plus there's a long list of festive activities and religious feasts taking place all over the island. As the inhabitants of the Canary Islands are deeply devoted to tradition, the origin of some of these fiestas goes back as far as Guanche times.

The majority of these fiestas are associated with the cult of saints, in particular patron saints. Or, in agricultural regions, they mark the end of harvest and are often celebrated with large and colourful processions or fancy-dress parades. Some of them even last from one to three weeks. Besides much entertainment and fun for young and old, these fiestas always offer a full programme of traditional activities, folklore performances, sporting events, such as lucha canaria wrestling and stick fighting competitions, and much more.

With all these fiestas happening around the island, you'd be very unlucky if you didn't come across at least one or two especially if you're visiting in summer. And if you're looking for a specific fiesta or festival, on this page you'll be able to find out more about some of the most important and most colourful events and when and where they are happening…

Around the Island
What's on around the Island

January/February

Dia de los Reyes Magos (Day of The Three Wise Men) - January 6th

This is a big day all over the island and Epiphany is celebrated with street parades in most cities. The Three Wise Men come to town on the evening of January 5th, where they give out sweets to children.

Fiesta del Almendro en Flor (Festival of the Almond in Blossom)

This fiesta takes places in early February when the almond trees are in bloom. Celebrated on a grand scale in the towns of Tejeda and Valsequillo, this festival also gives people the chance to taste local produce, such as almond wines and sweets, and to enjoy traditional folk dancing and singing.

February/March

Carnival around the island

In Gran Canaria, carnival is celebrated in almost every corner of the island and if you want to experience the most famous and exuberant, make your way to Las Palmas, San Bartolomé, Maspalomas, Agüimes, Agaete or Telde, each of these towns' carnival festivities having their own trademark. Dressing up in colourful costumes, dancing and singing are mainly what carnival is all about. Some people love carnival so much they travel around the island to follow the festivities there is always a great party atmosphere and much to see.

Enjoy the fantastic shows that include extensive programmes, generally starting with an opening speech (pregón), full of humour and irony. Then, during the weeks leading to the climax of the last carnival weekend before Ash Wednesday there are competitions for the 'murgas' (typical carnival bands who sing satirical and funny songs), 'comparsas' (Brazilian-like carnival dancers) and music groups mixed with many other events like drag queen competitions, comedy shows and much more.

Carnival officially ends with the beginning of Lent on Ash Wednesday, but this is Gran Canaria so head down to Playa del Inglés where the party continues with another weekend of processions and parties held mainly around the Yumbo Centrum.

March/April
Holy Week
During the Semana Santa the week before Easter you will be able to see solemn pre-Easter processions, where sacred icons and religious statues are carried through the streets of many villages and towns throughout the island.

April/May

Rally Islas Canarias Trofeo El Corte Inglés

This is Gran Canaria's biggest car rally. Attracting many international competitors, its stages include Ingenio to Tejeda, Artenara to Valleseco and Telde to Ayacata.

Fiesta de los Aborígenes April 29th

This feast day marks the final uprising of the Guanches against the Spaniards and the annexation of Gran Canaria by the Crown of Castile in 1483. There are big ceremonies taking place at Fortaleza Grande near Santa Lucía, as well as music and dancing events.

Fiestas del Queso April 27th May 4th

The small town of Santa María de Guía celebrates the making of its famous cheese with traditional music and dancing, along with plenty of cheese-eating.

Día de Canarias (Canary Islands' Day) May 30th

This is the official holiday for all the Canary Islands. There are celebrations in every corner, including concerts, the traditional Canarian wrestling, folk groups and more, mainly focusing on tradition.

Late May/early June

Corpus Christi

As an act of respect and religious devotion, streets and squares are decorated with beautiful carpets of flowers and in some areas dyed salt is used - a truly impressive display to create a colourful path for the processions. Las Palmas is usually the place to go for the best flower decorations in gran Canaria; a good starting point to visit many other towns and villages for a true feast of colour!

July

Fiesta del Carmen July 16th

The Virgen del Carmen is the patron saint of fishermen, that's why this celebration is so important in all the Canary Islands. This is especially so in Barrio de la Isleta, Las Palmas, Arguineguín and Puerto Mogán where this festivity can last up to one week and statues of the Virgin are taken out to sea in processions of decorated boats.

August

Bajada de la Rama (Bringing down the Branches) August 4th

This colourful fiesta, one of the oldest on the island, has its roots in the Guanches' rain dance and is held in Agaete. Nowadays, villagers carry pine branches from Agaete down to a chapel dedicated to the Virgen de Las Nieves. In the old times the aborigines would thrash the ocean waters with the branches to bring the rain in.

September

Fiesta de la Virgen del Pino September 8th

Every year, the Fiesta de la Virgen del Pino (Feast of Our Lady of the Pines) is celebrated and numerous pilgrims from all over the island come to Teror to pay reverence to the saint. This feast is not only the biggest event in the region it is also the most important religious festival on the island's calendar and the celebrations usually go on for one week.

Fiesta del Charco (Festival of the Lagoon) September 11th

The origins of this fiesta hark back to an aboriginal past. It is held in Puerto de la Aldea, a municipality of San Nicolás de Tolentino. Traditional rituals include villagers wading fully dressed in the lagoon, trying to catch fish with their bare hands and splashing each other with water.

October

Fiestas de la Naval (Festival of the Sea) October (2nd Saturday of the month)

Maritime processions in Las Palmas and other ports commemorate the victory of the Spanish Armada over the British explorer Sir Francis Drake in 1595.

December

Día de Santa Lucía December 13th

This winter festival combines Swedish and Canarian traditions and is principally celebrated in Santa Lucía de Tirajana in the southwest of the island.

Navidad December 25th

There are many traditions to be enjoyed and discovered during Christmas time in Gran Canaria and the nativities play an important role. The village of Veneguera (near Mogán) provides the stage for a popular nativity play on Christmas evening. Playa de las Canteras also organises a very different tradition with Nativity-related sand sculptures. Many international artists are invited and the results are truly spectacular.

New Year celebrations (Nochevieja) December 31st

The New Year celebrations (Nochevieja) usually start with dinner at a restaurant (book in advance, this is a big night) and plenty of fun, music and dancing. Make sure you get your lucky grapes! It is said you'll be lucky in the next year if you eat 12 grapes at midnight, one per stroke of the clock.

Las Palmas
What's on in Las Palmas

January/February

Cabalgata de los Reyes Magos (Parade of the Three Wise Men) January 5th

This is one of the most popular traditions related to Christmas time. On the eve of Epiphany, the 'Three Wizard Kings' from the Bible, ride camels through the streets of Las Palmas and are surrounded by floats. They throw sweets to the children and also receive their letters requesting gifts which are opened the following day. Often the Cabalgata de los Reyes helps to raise funds for children's charities.

Festival de Música de Canarias

Classic music concerts with international orchestras and soloists take place throughout the Canary Islands. Famous names to have graced the festival over the years include Sir Simon Rattle, Sir Georg Solti, Plácido Domingo and José Carreras.

February/March

Carnival in Las Palmas

The dates vary from year to year, but the main carnival celebrations last from three weeks to a month. One highlight is La Noche de la Sábana, a party where revellers wear little more than a sheet. Then there is a competition to elect the Carnival Queen, who is chosen in a big gala ceremony. A children's Carnival Queen is also chosen. All big events and parties centre around a large open-air stage in Santa Catalina Park.

During carnival, Las Palmas is home to one big party with Latin American music, brass bands, clowns, magicians, acrobats, fireworks and the noisy and colourful fancy-dress parades. Yet the wildest night of all is when the Carnival Drag Queen is chosen. The exuberant parade, led by the lavishly decorated float of the Carnival Queen, takes place the following day. It starts in La Isleta and continues for several hours on a set itinerary through the city to the big stage at Santa Catalina Park, ending at midnight with a big fancy-dress party, where everybody joins in.

The Children's Carnival is next to dominate the action. Finally, everything ends when the Entierro de la Sardina, Burial of the Sardine, takes place at Playa de las Canteras, accompanied by bonfires and fireworks. Apart from the residents of the city of Las Palmas and many people from other parts of the island, this carnival also attracts thousands of tourists each year.

March
Festival Internacional de Cine de Las Palmas (International Film Festival of Las Palmas)
Gran Canaria's film festival attracts many international movie stars.

The likes of Catherine Deneuve, Susan Sarandon and Vanessa Redgrave have visited in recent years. Films, including many independent movies, are screened in various places around the city.

March/June
Festival de Opera
This is an international opera festival, in which most of the Canary Islands participate, but it's principally held in Las Palmas' Teatro Pérez Galdós.

June
Festival Internacional de Música Popular
This is a folk music and dance festival with an international flavour, where both local and visiting groups perform.

San Juan (St. John's Day) June 24th
This day commemorates the foundation of the city of Las Palmas with pagan and Christian rituals and a big party. Bonfires are lit on the beaches on the night of June 24th, the high point of a week of concerts, theatre, dance and sports events, and many partygoers swim in the sea at Playa de las Canteras.

July

Festival Internacional Canarias Jazz & Más Heineken

This festival takes place during three weeks in July on all of the Canary Islands. On Gran Canaria it is staged in Las Palmas and includes jazz concerts performed by prominent international musicians.

Fiesta de Nuestra Señora del Carmen Mid-July

This fiesta is held in the middle of July, when the Puerto de la Luz harbour and the fishermen and residents of the district of La Isleta honour their patron saint. During this maritime procession, the figure of the Virgin is carried on the shoulders of a crowd of revellers from the parish church who then board a boat for her annual trip along the coast off the bay of Las Palmas. Particularly eye-catching are the carpets of fresh flowers in the streets, many of them made by the local residents for this special occasion.

October

Fiesta de la Naval Early October

Taking place in La Isleta district, this event, which is celebrated with a maritime procession, impressive flower decorations and fireworks, commemorates the victory of the island over the attacks from the British admirals Sir Francis Drake and John Hawkins in October 1595.

Romería de Nuestra Señora de la Luz

Romería de Nuestra Señora de la Luz (Pilgrimage in honour of Our

Lady of the Light) this feast is celebrated with a procession of decorated boats at sea to honour the Virgin.

November

Atlantic Rally for Cruisers (ARC)

Taking place on the last Sunday in November, this famous rally for yachts, departing from Las Palmas to the Caribbean, attracts many international participants.

WOMAD

This event runs over the course of four nights (Thursday to Sunday), although there are activities in the day for both children and adults. This festival draws some of the biggest names from world music. Previous performers who have graced the stages include the legendary Femi Kuti, Amadou & Mariam and Salif Keita.

Where to Stay

4 & 5 star Hotels & Resorts, Apartments, Villas and Hostels in Gran Canaria

Gran Canaria's fabulous climate and varied beaches attract visitors to its shores all year round, with the numerous resorts and hotels offering an abundance of facilities that aim to satisfy all travellers' needs. These resorts all offer varied entertainment, a good nightlife, beach amenities, plenty of shopping opportunities and a myriad of bars and restaurants, so how do you choose the location and hotel that suits you best?

Thanks to our local knowledge of the island, Spain-Grancanaria can help you narrow down your choices by recommending hotels in a variety of resorts, as well as apartments, hostels or villas, guaranteeing the best locations, the most competitive prices and high quality accommodation.

San Agustín, one of the island's first resorts, is a peaceful destination with a lovely long beach and home to the prestigious Hotel Meliá Tamarindos. This hotel houses the first casino to be built in the south of the island and is surrounded by manicured gardens that lead down to the beach. The nearby Gloria Palace San Agustín Thalasso & Hotel boasts the best thalassotherapy centre in Gran Canaria.

The adjoining resort of Playa del Inglés, the most well-known in Gran Canaria, is the most animated in the south of the island. Hotel Neptuno enjoys a central location near the Hard Rock Café, the Kasbah shopping centre and the popular gay venue, the Yumbo Centrum. Situated further inland, Vital Suites Hotel & Spa (formerly known as Dunas Vital Suites) overlooks the Maspalomas golf course in a quieter area of Playa del Inglés.

Maspalomas is a more peaceful resort and home to the glorious sand dunes and natural reserves of the lagoon and palm grove. The prestigious IFA Faro Hotel is situated at the very entrance to the beach.

The trendy resort of Meloneras lies just beyond the Faro lighthouse. More sophisticated than other resorts, it boasts casinos, exclusive shops and a scenic promenade. The Lopesan Costa Meloneras Resort Spa & Casino enjoys a central location near the lighthouse and promenade while the 5-star Lopesan Villa del Conde Resort & Corallium Thalasso offers fabulous sea views and a luxurious spa. The Lopesan Baobab Resort is situated just behind Meloneras and contains large recreational areas in its African-inspired surroundings that children will love.

Puerto Rico and Amadores have sheltered, golden-sand beaches. Marina Suites is in Puerto Rico's dynamic marina and harbour area and offers excellent family-friendly apartments and a superb infinity pool that overlooks the sea. The Amadores beach hotels, Gloria Palace Royal Hotel & Spa and Gloria Palace Amadores Thalasso & Hotel provide excellent sea views from their cliff-side vantage points.

Although a more isolated resort, Taurito's beach is complemented by its enormous 'Lago' salt-water swimming pool. The large complex of Hotel LTI Valle Taurito provides an extensive array of leisure activities.

Removed from the coast and located amidst the breathtaking mountains of the San Bartolomé de Tirajana valley, Hotel Rural Las Tirajanas offers stunning views and a number of hiking and mountaineering activities in this scenic part of the island.

In the capital of Las Palmas, the fabulous beach of Playa de Las Canteras is situated right next to the hub of the city's nightlife. It is bordered by a popular promenade, lined with a profusion of bars, restaurants, hotels and shops and is a favourite place for strolling. Hotel Cristina Las Palmas gives onto the beach. AC Gran Canaria is also very close to the beach and just around the corner from the popular Santa Catalina Park. Further removed from Las Canteras and situated amidst the exotic gardens of the Parque Doramas lies the elegant, colonially-inspired Hotel Santa Catalina.

Gran Canaria Hotels

Lopesan Villa Del Conde Resort
Delight in the luxury and local flavour of the Lopesan Villa del Conde Resort & Corallium Thalasso hotel in trendy Meloneras, where an

outstanding array of facilities, dazzling views, scenic walks, beautiful beaches and varied forms of entertainment await you.

Lopesan Baobab Resort
The exotic coast of Meloneras on Gran Canaria was waiting for such a hotel. The Lopesan Baobab Resort will not fail to impress you with the fantastic facilities and amenities around, creating the feeling of a true luxurious African Lodge.

Hotel Santa Catalina
The five-star Hotel Santa Catalina has become a landmark of Las Palmas on the island of Gran Canaria. The fantastic facilities close to the sports harbour provide everything for a relaxing holiday. Equally, if you're travelling on business, this hotel won't disappoint.

Hotel Cristina Las Palmas
Overlooking the lovely beach of Las Canteras and situated in the hub of the city's nightlife, recently refurbished Hotel Cristina Las Palmas offers a unique location, fabulous views and contemporary surroundings in the exciting city of Las Palmas.

Meliá Tamarindos
On the beachfront of San Agustín stands the five-star Meliá Tamarindos hotel. Its large glass windows fill its interiors with the bright Canarian light and look out onto the Atlantic, two swimming pools, a Mini Club and a fabulous spa; all ideal for your holiday.

Hotel Neptuno
Situated in the centre of the most animated part of Playa del Inglés and a short walk away from the fabulous beach and dunes, adults only Hotel Neptuno provides all the ingredients for an exciting holiday in the south of Gran Canaria.

Ac Hotel Gran Canaria
Set in the cosmopolitan city of Las Palmas, the AC Hotel Gran Canaria boasts a 4-star service and a great location. Just a step away from the Parque Santa Catalina and the Playa de las Canteras, splendid amenities, a roof-top pool and a restaurant complement the hotel.

Gloria Palace San Agustín Thalasso & Hotel
Enjoy the select atmosphere of San Agustín at the Gloria Palace San Agustín Thalasso & Hotel. Situated a short distance from the beach, this family-friendly hotel provides exceptional facilities and one of the most impressive thalassotherapy centres in Europe.

Ifa Faro Hotel
IFA Faro Hotel's enviable location overlooking the Maspalomas shoreline offers you incomparable views of the natural beauty for which this area is renowned and proximity to the entertainment and amenities of this resort and of nearby Meloneras.

Lopesan Costa Meloneras Resort

Experience the grandeur of the 4-star Lopesan Costa Meloneras Resort, Corallium Spa & Casino, boasting modern accommodation and beautiful tropical gardens in the south of Gran Canaria. Outstanding facilities include the hotel's inviting infinity pool, casino and superb spa.

Gloria Palace Amadores Thalasso & Hotel
The 4-star Gloria Palace Amadores Thalasso & Hotel will be perfect for your Gran Canaria trip. Fabulous sea views, inviting accommodation, 3 sea-facing pools and an exclusive thalassotherapy centre are just a start to the long list of fine facilities offered by this hotel.

Gloria Palace Royal Hotel & Spa
The 4-star superior Gloria Palace Royal Hotel & Spa has something for all! With two fantastic swimming pools overlooking the Playa Amadores, a spectacular spa, several sporting activities and special facilities for children, this is the ideal hotel for your holiday.

Hotel Paradise Valle Taurito
Experience an outstanding, all-inclusive holiday at Hotel Paradise Valle Taurito. The 4-star hotel in south-west Gran Canaria boasts elegant modern accommodation complemented by a wide range of resort-style leisure facilities for the whole family.

Hotel Rural Paradise Las Tirajanas

Visit the countryside gem of Gran Canaria - the Hotel Rural Paradise Las Tirajanas. Marking the centre of the island with its rustic-inspired architecture, this 4-star hotel set in the quaint village of San Bartolomé de Tirajana will be perfect for every nature-loving guest.

Marina Suites Hotel
Situated near the harbour in Puerto Rico, the elegant 4-star Marina Suites offers outstanding accommodation in the south of Gran Canaria. Boasting excellent facilities and modern self-catering suites, the hotel is only a short walk from lovely sun-drenched beaches.

Travel Information

Our guide spain-grancanaria.com has lots of travel information that will certainly be very useful when planning your trip to this island. We will explain you how to get to this holiday destination that belongs to an area of the Atlantic Ocean known as 'Macaronesia', which includes the Canary Islands, as well as the archipelagos of Madeira, Azores, Cape Verde and part of Morocco.

If you are wondering when to go to Gran Canaria, we can already tell you that any time of the year is good to visit this Spanish island. Besides telling you all about interesting places to visit, beaches, hotels and other essential information, this guide will also give you useful advice about getting around Gran Canaria, but first here are some data for you to have a geographical perspective: Gran Canaria is a volcanic island covering an area of 602 square miles (1,560 km²) with the highest peak being Pico de las Nieves at 6,394 feet (1,949 metres). Located in the Atlantic Ocean, 93 miles (150 kilometres) off the northwestern coast of Africa, the island is the third largest of the Canary Islands and has the most populated and dynamic capital city. Las Palmas is home to approximately 400,000 of the island's total population of 820,257.

Today, Gran Canaria enjoys 2.2 million visitors a year and is often referred to as a 'miniature continent' because of its different climates and variety of landscapes. In our 'What to bring' section, we'll give you some important tips, from documents to clothes, depending on what you plan to do.

By the way, did you know that one third of the island has been designated a protected Biosphere Reserve by the UNESCO? As you can see, this little piece of paradise awaits you!

When to get to Gran Canaria

Gran Canaria is often described as the 'island of eternal spring'. That is quite true. Gran Canaria is a year round destination and you can really come at any time without disappointment.

Of course during winter it does get a little cooler, but compared to central and northern Europe it is still pure paradise. Inevitably, the warm winter does tend to draw the bulk of tourists and December to February can definitely be considered 'high season'.

Not quite so busy, but certainly also a high season are the months between May and October. The cool sea breezes can be very refreshing compared to the 'scorchers' associated with mainland Spain.

Air fares are most attractive between November and mid December, also from March to May with the exception of Easter which is very popular indeed. Flights prices throughout August can also be more expensive because of the school holidays.

How to get to Gran Canaria

Planning a trip to Gran Canaria? Make sure you know what documents are required to get onto the island. The Canary Islands are an autonomous region within Spain. This means the same regulations apply when it comes to entering Gran Canaria. You must hold a valid passport or visa depending on what country you live in, the duration of your visit and your reason for travelling, e.g. tourism, work or study.

If you are at all unsure, please contact your travel agent or the Embassy/Consulate of Spain based in your hometown before you travel.

Gran Canaria enjoys scheduled flight connections with all the other islands of the archipelago and with mainland Spain. Many European cities also provide charter flights to Gran Canaria.

There are regular ferries and hydrofoil services to and from Tenerife, Lanzarote and Fuerteventura. Passengers arriving from these destinations and also from mainland Spain (Cádiz), dock at Puerto de la Luz in Las Palmas, in the north of the island. You can also travel to and from Funchal, the capital of Madeira, by ferry. If you are travelling with a caravan, please note that caravans are not allowed on campsites in Madeira.

Vaccinations

You do not need vaccinations to visit the Canary Islands, unless you are travelling from an infected area. If you are in any doubt, check with your tour operator or local Spanish Embassy.

Airport (LPA)

Gran Canaria is a popular holiday destination for many reasons, and millions of tourists from all over the world visit this wonderful 'miniature continent' every year. As you would expect, on an island fully prepared and geared towards tourism, good transport facilities are a key factor.

Located 18 km south of Las Palmas, Gran Canaria Airport opened in 1930. Nowadays, it is one of the busiest airports in Spain, operating with several companies and destinations. It is estimated that, for example, in 2014, this airport has handled over 10 million passengers!

Currently with two terminals, this airport is considered one of the safest in the world and, given the island's good weather conditions, it is open 24 hours a day, all year round, offering all the amenities you need, such as information desks.

This infrastructure is located 25 km from the tourist area of Gran Canaria (south zone) and 18 km from the capital, Las Palmas. The first thing you need to know after landing on Gran Canaria is how to get to your hotel or resort. From this airport you can go to any part of the island, since there are connections to different types of transport and services, such as buses, taxis, transfers and car rental.

Our convenient and stress-free transfer service guarantees peace of mind. A representative will welcome you at the airport and drive you directly to your hotel. If you choose to have your own vehicle, car rental prices on the Canary Islands are considerably lower than in mainland Spain. Generally, you will get a better price if you book in advance (Internet bookings are probably the most competitively priced). There are taxis available at the airport. Just look for off-white cars with a blue stripe on the sides of each front door. Other signs that might help you recognise a taxi are the letters SP (meaning Servicio Público) and a green light on top or in the front windscreen (which indicates that the taxi is empty). This is the quickest but most expensive option, and costs vary according to your final destination. There are frequent bus services between the airport and most of the resorts on the island. The journey to Las Palmas (in the north) takes around 35 minutes, while a bus ride to Playa del Inglés (in the south) will take around half an hour.

Services

Gran Canaria Airport has restaurants and cafes, ATMs, an amusement area for children, public telephones, free wifi, post office, currency exchange, conference rooms, lost and found area, medical services, pharmacies and shops (jewellery, tobacco stores, newspapers, perfumes, toys, clothing, etc.).

People with reduced mobility

In compliance with all airports in Europe, Gran Canaria Airport meets all the conditions for people with special needs, with a free assistance service. However, if special assistance is required, it is advisable to book it in advance with the airline. Facilities also include ramps, adapted elevators and parking spaces reserved for people with reduced mobility.

Luggage

This airport offers all the necessary services in the event of loss (Lost and Found), destruction or delay of checked baggage.

Hotels

Although at this airport there are no hotels, it is not difficult to find good hotels, hostels, apartments, resorts and guesthouses near this infrastructure. Click here to see our list.

Parking

The airport has two parking areas: one with a capacity of almost 1,500 vehicles, with a competitive price, located right next to the terminal and for short-term stays, and another for long-term parking, the ideal option for anyone going on holidays and needing a place to leave their vehicle.

Travelling from the airport to your destination by Bus

To and from the airport, lines 1, 5, 11, 36, 60, 66, 90 and 91, from 'Global' company, have several timetables. Line 1 travels between Las Palmas and Puerto de Mogán. A trip from the airport to Las Palmas costs €2.30, and from the airport to Puerto de Mogán costs €6.80. Line 5 connects Las Palmas to Faro de Maspalomas, with a trip from the airport to Faro de Maspalomas costing €4.05. Line 11 connects Las Palmas and Aguimes, and a trip between the airport and Aguimes has a cost of €1.40. With line 36, from Faro de Maspalomas to Telde, a trip from the airport to Telde has a cost of €1.45. In line 60, from Las Palmas to the airport, the trip costs €2.30. Line 66 connects Faro de Maspalomas to the airport (and vice versa), line 90 links Faro de Maspalomas to Telde, and line 91 makes the connection between Las Palmas and Playa del Cura. A trip between the airport and Patalavaca costs €5.25, and between the airport and Arguineguín has a cost of €4.95.

Travelling from the airport to your destination by Taxi

When leaving the airport, you will immediately find a taxi. The trip to Las Palmas costs around €30. A surcharge is added to overnight trips (between 22pm and 6am).

Car hire

To enjoy your holidays autonomously, rent a car at the best price at Discount Rent A Car. You will find a wide range of hire cars and get an instant quote.

What to Bring along

Are you one of those people who has a tendency to overpack? Well, Gran Canaria is the ideal destination for you: with bargain shopping in abundance, you can arrive practically naked and buy your fresh, new holiday attire here. However, we do advise that you bring the bare necessities... which for this sun-kissed island will mainly include sunglasses, swimwear, a high factor sun lotion and flip flops!

What you like to do on holiday will determine what you need to pack. If you like fine dining or clubbing, for instance, remember to bring some smarter clothes, as beachwear and trainers may not be accepted in some formal restaurants or nightclubs.

Many people like exploring, so if you are planning an adventure into the mountains or a day trip inland, take a light sweater to keep you warm. For the hikers among you, remember to bring practical footwear and some waterproof clothing might come in handy as the weather in mountainous areas can change quickly..

You may also need to bring general items including an electrical plug adapter — in Gran Canaria, you need a two-pin 220 volt plug. A driving licence is necessary if you want to hire a car and photo ID is needed when you pay by credit or debit card. Perhaps you want to try out your language skills and bring along a Spanish phrasebook too?

Getting Around

As the third largest island of the archipelago, Gran Canaria has many sightseeing options. And with so many things to see, you just have to choose your destination and the means of transport most convenient for you to tour the island. But first things first before you arrive in Gran Canaria, you can book online an airport transfer, choosing between a private car or a mini bus, that will pick you up at the airport to take you to the hotel, and vice versa at the end of your holidays.

If, during your stay, you would like to visit another island, such as Tenerife, Lanzarote or Fuerteventura, there are several ferry companies that can take you there. Renting a car or taking a taxi allows you to control your own schedules and always have a vehicle waiting for you. Should you prefer to enjoy the landscape through the window rather than behind the wheel, taking the public buses, commonly known as 'guaguas', is the most economical (but also the most time consuming) option to get around Gran Canaria.

Airport Transfer

Arriving at Gran Canaria Airport? Let Spain-Grancanaria transfers take you straight from the airport to your hotel or sun-drenched resort. Forget about expensive taxi fares and infrequent bus services simply book online before you go to ensure reliable and affordable transport to and from your accommodation. Just fill in your details, flight numbers and select from a limousine, private transfer or mini bus to take you direct to your door.

Whether you're visiting the capital of Las Palmas, staying in the popular oceanfront resorts of Playa del Inglés and Meloneras or holidaying in Puerto Mogán, our airport transfer service offers hassle-free transport so you can get straight to the beach! With so many lively resorts, natural attractions and activities for the whole family, Gran Canaria is a perfect destination for a holiday in the sun.

Gran Canaria Taxis

Having your own wheels is always the best way to explore any place, but just in case you're not in the mood to drive you can always search for a taxi. In the south they are easy to spot as they are white and have a distinctive red stripe on their front doors. They change colour depending on the location. In Las Palmas, for example, taxis are white with a blue stripe on the doors. Also, they display the letters SP (*Servicio Público*) with a green light on top or at the front of the car, indicating that the taxi is vacant and able to be hired.

Local journeys are metered and charges increase depending on what day of the week and time you use them. There is a basic rate Monday to Saturday from 6:00 to 22:00 and a more expensive rate from 22:00 to 06:00. Sundays and public holidays are also charged at a more expensive rate. If you're travelling outside municipal boundaries, make a point of arranging a fixed fare in advance. From the airport to Las Palmas, depending on the time of day and where you're staying, the fare will fluctuate. In the south of the island, where taxis belong to a local co-operative, using a cab is a good, inexpensive way to travel.

Car Hire

Low Cost Gran Canaria Car Hire

Spain-Grancanaria, your number one holiday tour operator has got everything covered... through Discount Rent A Car we can guarantee super savings, top quality service and a choice of thousands of vehicles, all of which are maintained to a very high standard.

There are many options, just choose the one that is most convenient. You can pick up your car in one location and return it to another completely free of charge or we will deliver it directly to your hotel. Needless to say, we are also represented at the airport.

Why rent a car from us?

Holidays are often the highlight of the year for many people. Everybody wants carefree, dependable car rentals at a reasonable price. This is exactly what you will get with us, which is why our clients return again and again

Driving in Gran Canaria

The driving laws for Gran Canaria are the same as in all Spanish territories. Motorists can hire a vehicle with a valid driving licence, passport/ID card and a credit card.

The new Traffic Reform Bill came into effect in May 2010 and introduces tougher rules for motorists. Under the new legislation, average-speed cameras are now legal in Spain. The camera measures the speed of a vehicle at two points and calculates the average. The camera is triggered if the legal speed limit is broken and a fine will be issued.

Handling a GPS while the vehicle is moving is classified as a serious offence and using a mobile phone is strictly forbidden, even if the car is stationary. To use a phone, motorists must pull off the road and be away from any other traffic.

The speed limit on motorways is 120 km/h, while in towns and cities it's 50 km/h, unless otherwise indicated. Parking is prohibited on white or yellow lines and blue lines indicate a restricted parking area where you must purchase a ticket from a pay-and-display machine. Parking in a disabled spot is against the law and could result in a fine.

Breath tests for alcohol are carried out randomly and non-residents may be subject to on-the-spot fines. The blood alcohol limit is 0.5 milligrams of alcohol per millilitre of blood (meaning 0.05% of alcohol detected in a blood sample). For drivers who have held their licence for less than two years, the limit is 0.1 milligram per milliliter (0.01%). Helmets are required when riding motorcycles or mopeds and the use of headphones when driving is strictly forbidden. Cyclists should wear a helmet and must have lights to ride in the dark.

In Gran Canaria they drive on the right-hand side of the road with steering wheels fitted on the left side of the car. The use of seatbelts in the front and back is compulsory. Children under the age of 12 may not travel in the front seats of the vehicle, unless they are more than 150cm in height.

Driving in the mountains can be a challenge with winding roads and narrow bends demanding the utmost concentration, so make sure to plan enough time for your journey. The only fast roads on the island are the GC1 motorway from Las Palmas to Arguineguín and the GC2 from Las Palmas to Agaete.

Necessary Info

Located in the Atlantic Ocean off the northwest coast of Africa, Gran Canaria enjoys a sub-tropical climate that promises great weather all year round. It has a population of approximately 820,000 (almost half of which live in the capital Las Palmas) and a total area of 1,560 sq. km. It is of volcanic origin and remains one of Spain's most popular holiday destinations.

At Spain-Grancanaria we believe in the old adage, knowledge is power. The more information you have the more prepared you are. It's our job to arm you with all the facts you'll need to make sure that you get the best from your holiday and avoid the dramas.

We understand that you may have questions and here you'll find the answers. Whether you want to know how to get to the airport, how to find tourist information offices or simply what kind of stuff to bring you'll find it on our pages. And should you wish to speak the language while you're away, check out our translation tips and glossary of key Spanish words.

If you do need a little extra help and guidance we have all the facts about medical care, insurances and emergency numbers which you are welcome to print off and take with you, just in case.

Maybe you're interested in Gran Canaria weather, the best places to see and things to do, maybe you want to know about the gay & lesbian scene or what the disabled facilities are like or even just how to say 'thank you', well we've got it covered here!

Currency

Banks and Currency

Spain inclusive of the Canary Islands introduced the Euro as legal tender in January 2002. The peseta ceased to be legal tender in June 2002. There are notes of 5, 10, 20, 50, 100, 200 and 500 Euros and coins of 1, 2, 5, 10, 20 and 50 cents, 1 and 2 Euros.

The use of major credit cards is widespread among local shops, making shopping easier. This is also the easiest way of having money without having to carry large amounts of cash, which minimises the damages in case of loss or theft. Credit card holders, and indeed debit card holders too, will need to present a valid picture ID however when purchasing goods with a card, like a driving licence or passport.

You will always require your passport to change money and banks will, without fail, charge a commission fee. Most hotels, travel agents and exchange offices - cambios - will also change your money but at a higher rate than the bank. You can also withdraw cash from an ATM using your credit or debit card (some banks will charge their clients for this service).

Travellers Cheques are safe and easily cashed at banks and exchange offices throughout Gran Canaria. Remember that you should keep the bank receipt listing the cheque numbers separate. If any of your cheques are stolen, this will be of great help.

Most banks usually open from Monday to Friday from 08.00 to 14.00. Some banks extend their opening hours one day in the week and some open on Saturday mornings too. Confusingly, there are also different opening hours during Christmas, Carnival times and in the summer.

Opening Hours in Gran Canaria

Shops in the Canary Islands keep different opening hours. The general rule is that larger shops, including department stores, fashion outlets and commercial centres, tend to open between 10.00 and 22.00 from Monday to Saturday.

Smaller shops, such as little supermarkets and convenience stores selling assorted items, either open at 9.00 or 10.00 and close at 13.00 for a lunch break, re-opening at 16.30 and closing at 20.30. However, stores in busy resorts can stay open until 22.00 or even later. Larger supermarkets open from 9.00 to 20.00.

Many governmental offices only open in the mornings. Apart from the major tourist resorts, shops remain closed on Sundays.

Museum opening times also vary and churches are totally unpredictable. Theme parks and gardens are generally open seven days a week and some close on public holidays.

Usually restaurants serve lunch between 13.00 and 16.00 and dinner between 20.00 and 23.00. Of course, there are some restaurants that stay open all day.

Now, a word of advice if you fancy going clubbing. Bear in mind that nightclubs do not get busy until much later than in most of Europe. Many people do not even turn up before 01.00 and the party goes on all night!

Electricity Information

The current used in Gran Canaria and throughout the Canary Islands is 220 Volts AC 50Hz and plugs have two round pins as found on the European continent.

Travellers from the USA will require a voltage converter, however the higher standard hotels do have provision for 110 Volt appliances like shavers.

Travellers from the UK will require a plug adapter and this is best bought in the UK as they are hard to find in the Canaries, although if you do forget El Corte Inglés department store is probably your best bet. Main sockets require round-pin plugs

Time & Water

The Canary Islands use the 24-hour clock, which can be quite confusing for those who are accustomed to 'am' & 'pm'.

Gran Canaria and its neighbouring islands maintain Greenwich Mean Time (GMT/UTC, which makes it identical to the UK but one hour behind most European countries and mainland Spain.

In March, the clocks are put forward one hour for daylight saving time. Clocks are put back one hour on the last Sunday in October.

Converting from AM/PM to the 24-hour clock:

between 12:00 AM and 12:59 AM, subtract 12 hours: 12:59 AM --> 00:59

between 1:00 AM and 12:59 PM, a straight conversion: 10:00 AM --> 10:00

between 1:00 PM and 11:59 PM, add 12 hours: 10:59 PM --> 2259

Converting from the 24-Hour clock to AM/PM:

between 00:00 and 00:59, add 12 hours: 00:59 --> 12:59 AM

between 01:00 and 11:59, straight conversion to AM: 01:00 --> 1:00 AM

between 12:00 and 12:59, straight conversion to PM: 12:59 --> 12:59 PM

between 13:00 and 23:59, subtract 12 hours: 15:59 --> 3:59 PM

We recommend that you do not drink tap water as it tends to be desalinated seawater. The locals almost all invariably drink bottled water.

Water from public fountains should not be drunk unless there is a sign saying Agua Potable. You will often see signs saying Agua No Potable, Water Not Drinkable. In bars, supermarkets or restaurants, ask for 'agua sin gas' (still) or 'agua con gas' (sparkling).

Some hotels do ask for co-operation when it comes to water consumption (for example, to put the towels out to wash every two days instead of doing it daily).

Dangers and Nuisances

In general, visitors should experience few problems travelling in the Canary Islands. The biggest threat Gran Canaria may pose is a bad case of sunburn or a nasty hangover! Regardless of the time of year that you choose to visit Gran Canaria, don't be fooled by cool breezes and cloudy days. Make the most of the glorious sunshine but remember to use a high factor sun lotion and apply it regularly. Also, drink plenty of water to keep hydrated.

Gran Canaria is a great place to party and there are lots of resorts where you can do just that. If you are looking for a more relaxed and peaceful holiday then head for tranquil places on the island.

If you hire a car, please remember not to leave anything of value inside, even if it is locked away in the boot. Use the safe in your hotel to secure passports, money and valuables; don't leave camera equipment or bags unattended and just like you wouldn't back home, avoid strange areas or anywhere that doesn't feel 'right'. In the event that something happens, file a report at the nearest police station and keep a copy for your insurance company. If your passport is lost, contact your consulate to get a replacement issued.

Our tip:
A backpack which zips up is a pretty safe way to carry your belongings but a concealed money belt or shoulder wallet will certainly keep your money and documents well hidden.

Health

Health and Medical Care in Gran Canaria

A wide selection of clinics and hospitals offer high-quality medical care, both private and national. The people from Gran Canaria are very health conscious indeed.

The Canary Islands are not renowned (thankfully) for any particular diseases and the worst you can get is a hangover from too much partying. It's very important to be aware of the risks from sunburn, dehydration or insect bites.

Many people visit Gran Canaria for its celebrated therapeutic value. It's especially popular with residents of European countries with colder weather that visit looking for relief from ailments such as arthritis and MS. People with mobility problems should always check they have booked accommodation in the flatter parts of the island.

Medical insurance is strongly advised, even though EU citizens who hold an EHIC (European Health Insurance Card) are entitled to basic national healthcare as received by local residents. You can apply for this online: https://www.ehic.org.uk/Internet/home.do.

There are many English-speaking doctors and dentists. Your hotel will always be able to recommend one. Visitors to the south would be well advised, however, to contact the British Medical Clinic in Puerto Rico

(+34 928 560 016). As well as offering private medical services, they offer translations of any tests you may have taken at a Spanish surgery or hospital.

The local chemists (farmacias), recognisable by a green cross sign, will have just about anything you may require and there is always one open after hours in each area. The location of the duty chemist is indicated on every chemist's door.

There are two main hospitals in Las Palmas. You'll find the older Hospital Insular on the Avenida Marítima del Sur, just as you leave Las Palmas heading in the direction of the airport and the south. There's also the newer Hospital Doctor Negrin, located closer to the Canteras beach. Elsewhere, Calle León y Castillo 231 houses the main Red Cross centre

Emergency Telephone Numbers

In case of an emergency, the local authorities can be contacted at the following numbers:

- Emergencies All islands 112
- Ambulance Dial 112 and the operator will put you through
- Police Station 091

- Hospital Doctor Negrín 928 45 00 00
- Hospital Insular 928 44 40 00
- Red Cross 928 22 22 22
- Fire Brigade Dial 112 and the operator will put you through

Communications

Communications in Gran Canaria

International telephone calls can be made from almost anywhere in the Canary Islands. Can't miss the distinctive blue booths and you'll have the choice of using coins, phone cards (*tarjetas telefónicas*) and sometimes credit cards. The country code for Gran Canaria is the same as Spain (34) followed by a nine-digit number usually starting with 928. Telephone calls made from bars, restaurants and hotels are usually a great deal more expensive than the street pay booths. The cheap rate for international calls is the night tariff from 22.00 to 08.00 and all day Sunday.

The Post Offices are open from 09.00 to 14.00 and close an hour earlier on Saturdays. There are no telephones in Post Offices. They do have stamps but so do tobacconists and other shops that sell postcards. Postboxes are yellow in colour but the service is quite laid-back. If you have important or urgent mail, we recommend you use one of the international courier companies instead.

Internet Cafés

There are a number of Internet cafés on the island and access costs around 2,00 Euro per hour. If you are travelling with your laptop and need access to a phone connection, be wary of using hotel-room outlets - the PABX system could destroy your processor. Jacks like those used in the US are standard and make connecting your modem simple. Also, most hotels in Gran Canaria offer a wifi connection free of charge.

Speaking Spanish

¿Hablas Español? Do you speak Spanish? Although the Canary Islanders speak Castellano, the accent you'll hear has more in common with the Spanish of Latin America in the South American countries of Cuba, Venezuela and Puerto Rico as opposed to the peninsular Spanish of mainland Spain. And it's not just an accent they share with South America but a rich vocabulary too - a living testament of the deep-lying associations formed by the various movements of people between the Canaries and the Latin American countries.

Ordinarily, Canarians will not pronounce the final 's' of a word. Neither will they pronounce the 'z' as 'th', as they do on the Spanish mainland, but rather as an 's'. And they pronounce a 'c' before 'i' or 'e' as a 's'. Canarians also often shorten words and sometimes even run them together in a sentence, which only serves to confuse the visiting listener more.

Although the indigenous Guanche language is now extinct, several words have survived, particularly when it comes to names of places. These often begin with the letters 'gua', pronounced 'wah'. You're more likely to hear local dialects in the countryside than in the cities or larger towns. Yet, visitors should avoid trying to learn the local dialect and instead stick to mainland Spanish. And if your Spanish is not quite 'up to it', the majority of Canarians you'll encounter will possess a basic knowledge of English, and most western European languages, but especially French, German, Italian and Portuguese.

If you're travelling away from the major resorts or urban districts, it's well worth taking along a small Spanish-English dictionary or phrase book. Also, the Internet serves as a rich resource for learning the lingo. There are a multitude of sites for you to discover essential Spanish vocabulary, as well as plenty with translation tools.

Below is our handy glossary section where you'll find some Spanish expressions and words which could come in useful:

Desayuno Breakfast	Malo Bad
Comida (de Mediodía) Lunch	Cerrado Closed
Cena Dinner	Abierto Open
Camarero/Camarera Waiter/Waitress	Aeropuerto Airport
No entiendo I don't understand	Oficina de Correos Post Office
Cuánto es/Cuánto vale/Cuánto cuesta? How much is it?	Farmacia Chemist
Escríbamelo, por favor Please write it down	Finca Rural Property
Sí Yes	Calle Street
No No	Ciudad Town/City
Buenos días Good morning	Gasolina Petrol
Buenas tardes Good afternoon/early evening	Alquiler to hire
Buenas noches Good evening/night	Alto/Pare stop
Por favor Please	Camino cerrado Road closed
Perdóneme Excuse me	Ceda el paso Give way
Habla usted Inglés? Do you speak English?	Coche Car
Dónde está...? Where is...?	Encrucijada crossroads
A qué distancia? How far?	Cuidado Warning
De nada You're welcome	Derecha Right
Gracias Thank you	Izquierdo Left
Adios Goodbye	Arriba Up
Hasta Luego So Long	Bajo Down
Bienvenido Welcome	Salida Exit
Bueno Good	Semáforo Traffic lights

The Gay & Lesbian

Gran Canaria boasts one of the largest and most vibrant gay and lesbian scenes in Europe. The most popular hotspots can be found around Playa del Inglés and Maspalomas.

For many years, the Yumbo Centrum has been the epicentre of nightlife and entertainment with over 50 venues including bars, restaurants, nightclubs and cabaret shows. Originally one of the island's first commercial centres, it is a multi-level shopping complex by day, full of boutiques and tourist outlets; at night, the place really comes alive and is bustling with plenty music and dancing. Colourful rainbow flags are proudly displayed, vivacious drag queens perform in bars and the mood is open, friendly and very welcoming. A night out here promises to be an entertaining experience for everyone.

Every year in May, Gay Pride Maspalomas is celebrated in and around the area of the Yumbo Centrum. It all started in 2001 as a way of honouring the island's gay community and similar parades are held worldwide. The week-long festivities include singers, performers and internationally renowned DJs, culminating in a large carnival procession on the last day. Visitors from all over the world travel to Gran Canaria to take part and soak up the atmosphere

Disabled Facilities

There are good facilities for the disabled at all the terminals of Gran Canaria airport including lifts, ramps and disabled spaces of all levels of the car park. In addition, Gran Canaria's major resorts of Playa del Inglés, Maspalomas, Meloneras, Puerto Rico and Mogán boast a selection of hotels with disabled-adapted rooms that are wheelchair friendly. Many include wheel-in showers and pool hoists. There has been recent investment in extensive promenade development along the coast in the south, which is now complete and is easily accessible for wheelchair and mobility scooter users.

All of the commercial centres have good access ramps to restaurants, bars and shops and the pavements are now better suited for wheelchair users than in the past. However, many of the older small bars and restaurants are still lacking in ramps and disabled facilities and although changing, it is happening slowly!

Adapted taxis with electric wheelchair lifts are available for airport transfers and short trips in Playa del Inglés, Maspalomas and Meloneras. Contact Socomtaxi on 928 154 777, for further details. Other island areas now have adapted taxis too, as well as estate cars and some seven-seated vehicles where a wheelchair can be carried in the boot. Disabled travellers are also advised to give SolMobility, a specialist firm based in Gran Canaria, a try. Providing 8-seater minibuses, these vehicles come fitted with electric wheelchair accessible lifts perfect for airport transfers and day excursions.

You can contact SolMobility S. L through www.SolMobility.com or by phone on (0034) 928 735 311. The recommended service provider to UK charities, tour operators, hotels and clinics of disabled-mobility aids, offer a wide-ranging selection of equipment with a free delivery & collection service to your hotel. On their website, you can find a list of hotels with adapted rooms that are wheelchair friendly. When planning a visit to Gran Canaria, disabled tourists should check the travel conditions and latest hotel facilities with their travel agent.

The Spanish association for the disabled *Confederación Española de Personas con Discapacidad Física y Orgánica* (COCEMFE) & Cruz Roja Española, Asamblea Local Las Palmas, León y Castillo, 231 35005 - Tel: 928 290 000 can help with emergencies. However, they will often only speak Spanish and it is a better idea to contact your tour operator directly for assistance.

Our tip:

Visit Holiday Care, the UK's Premier Holiday & Travel Information Service for Disabled and Older People, to buy a guide for the Canaries with very useful information online. Alternatively, contact them on 0845 124 9971.

Weather

Annual Weather and Climate for Gran Canaria

The trade winds, the Gulf Stream and Gran Canaria's geography have blessed this island with a wonderfully mild climate year-round, making it a great holiday destination and just a step away from mainland Europe.

In terms of annual weather, you can see in our weather charts that the average maximum temperatures remain very consistent throughout the seasons, ranging from 25 ºC and 28 ºC in summer (June, July and August) and between 21 and 22 ºC in the winter months (December, January and February).

March marks the beginning of spring and is a unique occasion to visit the capital, Las Palmas, where the International Film Festival is held. Although temperatures in Gran Canaria are pleasant throughout the year, they begin to increase in April and May.

The weather in the autumn months of September, October and November is quite similar to spring, although warmer and with a bit more rain.

And that's not all. At any given time of the year you will be able to enjoy several and very different microclimates depending on where you are — the coast, the interior or the mountains.

Sometimes, you can see snow in the highest peaks and you just need to travel down to the coast to spend the rest of your day basking under the sun — from subtropical to continental climates in one day!

Annual Average Temperatures for Gran Canaria

With a rich variety of microclimates, Gran Canaria is often described as a continent in miniature. Its position in the Atlantic Ocean ensures that this holiday hotspot enjoys spring-like temperatures all year round, with mild differences between the summer and winter months.

Summer temperatures average 26 ºC to 28 ºC (79 82 °F), and sometimes exceed 30 °C (86 °F). In winter, daytime temperatures can range from 16 ºC to 24 ºC (61 75 °F) with much cooler nights.

Gran Canaria is a mountainous island where the trade winds prevail all year. Rainfall is very rare in the summer months, falling at an average of 21 days per year, mostly over the winter period. Sometimes, you can see snow on the highest peaks while the coast is bathed in sunshine.

Gran Canaria

With 2,805 hours of sunshine annually, this is one of the sunniest places in the world. It's so easy to book your dream holiday in Gran Canaria.

www.ingramcontent.com/pod-product-compliance
Lightning Source LLC
Chambersburg PA
CBHW021058080526
44587CB00010B/297